EVERY STUDENT'S HANDBOOK

With Special Caribbean Material

Compiled by
Mike Henry

LMH Publishing Limited

© 2004 LMH Publishing Ltd.
10 9 8 7 6 5 4 3
New Edition
2007

Executive Editor: Charles Moore (LMH Publishing)

Cover Design by: Marcia Evans (Lee Quee Design)

Edited by: Rose Lewis Stone (Freelance Editor)

Typesetting by: Michelle Mitchell (PAGE Services)

Published by: LMH Publishing Limited
7 Norman Road,
LOJ Industrial Complex,
Building 10,
Kingston C.S.O., Jamaica.
Tel: 876-938-0005; 938-0712
Fax: 876-759-8752
Email: lmhbookpublishing@cwjamaica.com
Website: www.lmhpublishingjamaica.com

Printed in USA   ISBN   978-976-8202-45-1

PREFACE

Students are faced with many challenges. The changing world in which we live makes it necessary to keep up with new trends and the changing aspects of modern society. At the same time, it is also important to have a sound knowledge of society's traditions and the conventions which allowed it to function effectively. They are expected to have this knowledge, but are not always provided with the tools to extract it.

In this new edition of *Every Student's Handbook*, it is hoped that student's will be able to transcend the boundaries of academics into a broader knowledge of the world, popular personalities, mathematical formulas, world history, editing symbols and much more. The aim of this text is to supplement (not replace) attempts by teachers to educate and, as such, recommends itself as a handy classroom tool and reference guide for professionals in various fields.

We hope that you find this revised edition of *Every Student's Handbook* critical to the development of rounded students and teachers.

CONTENTS

SECTION ONE

ENGLISH

A. Revision Notes

PARTS OF SPEECH

Noun — A word that names a person, animal, place, thing or idea.
Adjective — A word that describes a noun.
Verb — A word that expresses an action or a state of being.
Adverb — A word that adds meaning to a verb, an adjective or another adverb.

Noun	Adjective	Verb	Adverb
ability	able	enable	ably
abuse, abusiveness	abusive	abuse	abusively
accommodation	accommodating	accommodate	accommodatingly
anger	angry	anger	angrily
applause	applausive	applaud	applausively
art	artistic	—	artistically
athlete	athletic	—	athletically
beauty	beautiful	beautify	beautifully
benefit	beneficial	benefit	beneficially
blind	blind	blind	blindly
breadth	broad	broaden	broadly
breath	breathless	breathe	breathlessly
brilliance	brilliant	—	brilliantly
caution	cautious	caution	cautiously
child, childhood	childish	—	childishly
circle	circular	circle	circlewise
clearness	clear	clear	clearly
comic	comical	—	comically
custom	customary	accustom	customarily
dark	dark	darken	darkly
depth	deep	deepen	deep, deeply
design	—	design	designedly

Noun	Adjective	Verb	Adverb
difference	different	differ	differently
dream	dreamy	dream	dreamily
dryer	dry	dry	drily
ease	easy	ease	easily
effect	effective	effect	effectively
error	erroneous	err	erroneously
eternity	eternal	eternalize	eternally
evidence	evident	evidence	evidently
falsehood	false	falsify	falsely
fame	famous	fame	famously
favour	favourable	favour	favourably
fool	foolish	fool	foolishly
freedom	free	free	freely
friend, friendship	friendly	friend	friendly
gaiety	gay	—	gaily
gain	gainful	gain	gainfully
general	general	generalize	generally
glare	glaring	glare	glaringly
gold	golden	gild	—
grace	gracious	grace	graciously
hard	hard	harden	hard
help	helpful	help	helpfully
honesty	honest	—	honestly
hope	hopeful	hope	hopefully
humour	humorous	humour	humorously
hunger	hungry	hunger	hungrily
ideal	ideal	—	ideally
idleness	idle	idle	idly
ignorance	ignorant	ignore	ignorantly
imagination	imaginative	imagine	imaginatively
injury	injurious	injure	injuriously
invitation	inviting	invite	invitingly
jar	jarring	jar	jarringly
jauntiness	jaunty	jaunt	jauntily

2

Noun	Adjective	Verb	Adverb
jest	jesting	jest	jestingly
judge, judgement	judicial	judge	judicially
jump	jumpy	jump	—
justice	just	justify	just
keenness	keen	—	keenly
kindness	kind	—	kindly
king, kingdom	kingly	king	kingly
knave	knavish	—	knavishly
kneading	kneadable	knead	—
knowledge	knowing	know	knowingly
laugh, laughter	laughing	laugh	laughingly
length	lengthy	lengthen	lengthily
less	less	lessen	less
liberty	liberal	liberate	liberally
loyalty	loyal	loyalize	loyally
magnet	magnetic	magnetize	magnetically
memory	memorable	memorize	memorably
metal	metallic	metallize	metallically
modern	modern	modernize	modernly
mother	motherly	mother	—
mourning	mournful	mourn	mournfully
name	nameless	name	namely
nation	national	nationalize	nationally
neglect, negligence	negligent	neglect	negligently
note	notable	note	notably
notice	noticeable	notice	noticeably
number, numeral	numeral, numerical	number	numerically
obedience	obedient	obey	obediently
objection	objectionable	object	objectionably
obligingness	obliging	oblige	obligingly
obscurity	obscure	obscure	obscurely
official	official	officiate	officially
open	open	open	openly
pardon	pardonable	pardon	pardonably

3

Noun	Adjective	Verb	Adverb
performance	performing	perform	—
pleasure	pleasing	please	pleasingly
popularity	popular	popularize	popularly
prophecy	prophetic	prophesy	prophetically
purity	pure	purify	purely
quantity	quantitative	quantify	quantitatively
quarrel	quarrelsome	quarrel	quarrelsomely
quaver	quavery	quaver	quaveringly
question	questionable	question	questionably
quick	quick	quicken	quick, quickly
quiet	quiet	quieten	quietly
radiance	radiant	radiate	radiantly
recognition	recognizable	recognize	recognizably
repeat	repeatable, repeated	repeat	repeatedly
response	responsive	respond	responsively
risk	risky	risk	riskily
ruin	ruinous	ruin	ruinously
smoke	smoky	smoke	smokily
society	sociable, social	socialize	socially
solid	solid	solidify	solidly
study	studious	study	studiously
submission	submissive	submit	submissively
sweet	sweet	sweeten	sweetly
talk	talkative	talk	talkatively
terror	terrible	terrify	terribly
tide	tidal	tide	tidally
title	titular	entitle	titularly
trouble	troublesome	trouble	troublesomely
trust	trusting	trust	trustingly
understanding	understanding	understand	understandingly
undulation	undulating	undulate	undulatingly
uniformity	uniform	uniform	uniformly
unity	united	unite	unitedly
upset	upset	upset	—
use	useful	use	usefully

Noun	Adjective	Verb	Adverb
vacancy	vacant	vacate	vacantly
value, valuable	valuable	value	valuably
vapour	vapourish	vaporize	vaporously
variable, variation	variable	vary	variably
vexation	vexing	vex	vexingly
vitality	vital	vitalize	vitally
waste	wasteful	waste	wastefully
watch	watchful	watch	watchfully
weariness	weary	weary	wearily
wind	windy	wind	windily
worth	worthy	worth	worthily
writing	written	write	—
yearning	yearning	yearn	yearningly
yield	yielding	yield	yieldingly
zeal	zealous	—	zealously
zigzag	zigzag	zigzag	zigzag

GENDER

In grammar, gender is classified under four headings:

1. MASCULINE gender, which indicates the male sex, e.g. father, son
2. FEMININE gender, which indicates the female sex, e.g. mother, daughter
3. COMMON gender, which indicates either sex, e.g. teacher, pupil
4. NEUTER gender, which indicates objects without sex, e.g. table, bicycle

The feminine gender is distinguished from the masculine gender in three ways:

(a) By the addition or omission of or change in the suffix.

Masculine	Feminine	Masculine	Feminine
actor	actress	heir	heiress
aviator	aviatrix	hero	heroine
bridegroom	bride	lad	lass
count	countess	mayor	mayoress
czar	czarina	sultan	sultana

Masculine	Feminine	Masculine	Feminine
duke	duchess	viscount	viscountess
emperor	empress	waiter	waitress
executor	executrix	widower	widow

(*b*) By a change in the prefix of a compound word.

Masculine	Feminine	Masculine	Feminine
billy-goat	nanny-goat	cock-sparrow	hen-sparrow
buck-rabbit	doe-rabbit	jack-ass	jenny-ass
bull-calf	cow-calf		

(*c*) By an entirely different noun.

Masculine	Feminine	Masculine	Feminine
bachelor	spinster	nephew	niece
boar	sow	ram	ewe
bullock	heifer	sir	madam
colt	filly	sire	dame
drake	duck	stallion	mare
drone	bee	swain	nymph
earl	countess	tutor	governess
fox	vixen	uncle	aunt
gander	goose	wizard	witch

FORMING POSSESSIVES

Singular Nouns

1. For a singular noun, the possessive case is formed by adding apostrophe *s*. ('s).

   the neighbour's dog · the priest's robes
   the milkman's van · the child's toys

2. For an abstract noun ending in *ss* or *ce,* only the apostrophe (') is added.

   for goodness' sake · for conscience' sake

3. For proper nouns ending with *s,* only the apostrophe (') is added.

   James' bag · Lewis' shirt

6

Plural Nouns

1. For a plural noun ending in *s* only the apostrophe (') is added.

the boys' marbles   the girls' dolls
the boxers' gloves   the students' books

2. If the plural noun does not end in *s*, the apostrophe *s* ('s) is added.

the children's clothes   the fishermen's nets
the women's jewellery   the men's shoes

Compound Nouns

1. For a compound noun, the possessive is added to the last word of the noun.

Singular	**Plural**
her mother-in-law's antiques	the businessmen's donations
the editor-in-chief's report	the postmasters' recommendations

ANTONYMS AND SYNONYMS

An antonym is a word opposite in meaning to another word.
A synonym is a word similar in meaning to another word.

ANTONYMS

abandon   —   keep, remain, stay
absence   —   presence, attendance
accord   —   discord, conflict, disagreement
arrive   —   depart, abscond, leave
assemble   —   disperse, disband, separate

big   —   little, small, petite
brave   —   cowardly, fearful
bright   —   dim, dark, dull

calm   —   tempestuous, tumultuous, stormy
capture   —   liberate, release, discharge
censure   —   praise, commend, laud
constant   —   changeable, unstable, inconsistent
converge   —   diverge, deviate, digress

damage	—	improve, protect, repair
deceitful	—	honesty, trustworthy, sincere
difficult	—	easy, unproblematic, uncomplicated
economic	—	extravagance, profligacy, lavishness
empty	—	full, occupied
entrance	—	exit, outlet
exact	—	inexact, imprecise, approximate
fail	—	succeed, thrive
foolish	—	wise, prudent, intelligent
frugal	—	spendthrift, wasteful, extravagant
gain	—	decrease, diminish, lessen
gay	—	miserable, despondent
give	—	receive, take, obtain
good	—	bad, poor, substandard
hoist	—	lower, descend
hollow	—	solid,
humorous	—	solemn, serious, formal
ignorant	—	knowledgeable, learned, well- informed
immediately	—	presently, currently
impoverish	—	enrich, supplement, enhance
inferior	—	superior, better-quality
innocent	—	guilty, culpable, liable
join	—	separate, divide, split
keen	—	dull
keep	—	lose, misplace
kind	—	cruel, unkind, vindictive
lag	—	hasten, hurry, rush
mad	—	sensible, sound, sane
melt	—	freeze, chill, solidify
native	—	alien, imported, foreigner
obedient	—	disobedient, unruly, insubordinate
offer	—	withhold, deny, refuse
old	—	young, juvenile,
open	—	close, shut, lock
oral	—	written, printed

8

pain	—	pleasure, joy, delight
past	—	present, current, now
play	—	work, toil, labour
quell	—	rouse, agitate, disquiet
question	—	answer, reply, respond
real	—	artificial, synthetic, false
reveal	—	conceal, hide, cover
safe	—	dangerous, risky, chancy
same	—	different, dissimilar, unlike
temporary	—	permanent, lasting, timeless
uniform	—	irregular, inconsistent
variation	—	sameness, similarity
warp	—	straighten
whole	—	part, fraction, piece
yield	—	resist, oppose, defy

SYNONYMS

abandon	—	desert, relinquish, renounce, leave
abide	—	tarry, live, endure
ability	—	proficiency, capability
accept	—	concede, acknowledge
accord	—	concur, grant
adjust	—	consummate, effect, realize
ado	—	flurry, bustle
bad	—	corrupt, evil, wicked, base
balance	—	poise, composure
balk	—	check, retard, impede
below	—	under, beneath
big	—	large, huge, immense, capacious, bulky
blame	—	reproach, reprove, condemn
body	—	carcass, corpse, cadaver
break	—	fracture, splinter, crush, shatter, smash
bright	—	refulgent, lustrous, lucent, radiant, clever

call	—	invite, summon
calm	—	still, quiet, motionless, placid, assuage, cool
capture	—	catch, apprehend, nab, arrest
careful	—	watchful, discreet, wary, meticulous, concerned, heedful
censure	—	reprove, reprimand, rebuke, chide
change	—	transmute, vary, alter, replace, trade, convert
character	—	individuality, reputation, personality
choice	—	alternative, option, rare
competent	—	fit, qualified, capable, able
constant	—	permanent, perpetual, incessant, loyal, steady

damage	—	harm, hurt, maim
deceit	—	deception, trickery
delay	—	detain, procrastinate, respite
difficult	—	arduous, hard, complex, fussy, obdurate
discharge	—	unburden, expel, release, perform

ebb	—	wane, subside, abate, recede
economical	—	sparing, thrifty, frugal
educate	—	teach, instruct, school, drill, indoctrinate
elevate	—	lift, promote, exalt
embarrass	—	discompose, chagrin, hamper
empty	—	vacuous, blank, void
envious	—	jealous, covetous
erect	—	standing, vertical, upright
event	—	happening, affair, episode, occurrence
exact	—	rigid, severe, scrupulous, accurate, correct
excuse	—	forgive, pardon, free

fail	—	decline, fade, disappoint, neglect
fancy	—	fantasy, idea, thought; fine, elegant, ornate
fate	—	karma, destiny, predestination
fault	—	blemish, foible, weakness
fear	—	apprehension, terror, panic, alarm, dread, concern
feed	—	nourish, sustain; fodder
fiction	—	fable, fantasy, figment
fight	—	encounter, affray, skirmish, melee, tussle, row, conflict
flash	—	flare, gleam, glint, glitter
flock	—	bevy, covey, gaggle, brood, herd, pack
fool	—	dolt, dunce, blockhead, ninny; delude, hoax
frugal	—	thrifty, chary, provident, penurious, stingy

gain	—	procure, get, attain, earn, win
gay	—	jovial, glad, cheerful, happy
get	—	obtain, acquire, procure, secure, win
give	—	offer, accord, furnish
good	—	pure, moral, upright, exemplary, benevolent, efficient, expert
graphic	—	striking, vivid, detailed
guise	—	form, shape
habit	—	bent, custom; dress, garb
hard	—	rigid, inflexible, exhausting, complex, onerous, severe, stern, unkind
harsh	—	brusque, brutal, rough, dissonant
heroic	—	valiant, gallant, brave
hoist	—	elevate, raise
humorous	—	laughable, jocose, comical, facetious
ideal	—	perfect, complete
ignorant	—	untutored, illiterate, uneducated
imbibe	—	drink, absorb
immediately	—	forthwith, directly, instantly, presently
impotent	—	powerless, helpless, feeble, weak
impoverish	—	deplete, drain, weaken, enervate
inconsistent	—	incoherent, incompatible, discrepant
innocent	—	sinless, virtuous, blameless, guileless, simple
join	—	link, couple, fasten, attach, combine, consolidate
jump	—	leap, vault, spring, hop
keen	—	sharp, cutting, caustic, earnest, fervid
keep	—	reserve, retain, hold, confine
kind	—	mild, gracious, humane, tender, benign
lag	—	loiter, linger
language	—	speech, tongue, dialect, vernacular, lingo
lease	—	rent, charter, hire
likely	—	apt, liable
little	—	tiny, teeny, diminutive, small
mad	—	lunatic, crazy; furious, irate, raging
magnificent	—	luxurious, exquisite, gorgeous, superb, splendid
manage	—	arrange, contrive, guide, handle
mandate	—	fiat, decree, edict, ruling

mass	—	aggregate, heap, pile; majority, proletariat; gather, collect
meaning	—	tenor, gist, drift, trend, sense
meet	—	confront, connect, cross, converge; settle, contest; appropriate; experience
melt	—	dissolve, thaw, fuse
muster	—	convoke, gather, convene, assemble, summon
nag	—	pester, harass, hector, irritate, vex
native	—	inherent, innate, inbred; natural, original, indigenous
noble	—	high-born, lofty, honourable, grand, splendid
noise	—	tumult, clamour, din, hubbub
obedient	—	compliant, docile, tractable, respectful
obscene	—	pornographic, smutty, filthy, lubricious
occupation	—	vocation, pursuit, craft, business
offer	—	proffer, tender, give, propose
old	—	aged, elderly
opening	—	orifice, slit, rift, chasm, fissure
organic	—	inherent, essential
pain	—	agony, anguish, torment, twinge
pant	—	gasp, thirst, hunger, yearn
parade	—	show, flaunt, flourish
parasite	—	sycophant, toady, leech, hanger-on
piece	—	section, scrap, fragment
play	—	show, diversion, sport; enact, impersonate
polish	—	shine, brighten, smoothen, refine
popular	—	favourite, liked, common
presage	—	indication, premonition, portent, sign
proper	—	suitable, befitting, decent, polite
prove	—	demonstrate, confirm, substantiate, verify
quell	—	crush, overpower, defeat
question	—	query, examine
raid	—	seizure, incursion, invasion, inroad
rash	—	hasty, impetuous, reckless, indiscreet
ravage	—	ruin, waste, devastate, despoil, plunder
real	—	actual, true, authentic
rebut	—	disprove, confute
recall	—	remember, rescind, retract, revoke, repeal
refer	—	attribute, ascribe, impute, allude

12

regard	—	respect, revere, value, notice, heed
regulate	—	moderate, control, adjust
remain	—	abide, stay, wait, tarry
riot	—	disorder, brawl, fray, disturbance
safe	—	protected, secure, reliable, sure
same	—	similar, like, equal, identical
scan	—	study, examine, scruitinize
scatter	—	dispel, disperse, dissipate, diffuse
search	—	investigate, examine, scrutinize
separate	—	sever, divide, disengage
shake	—	waver, tremble, vibrate, shiver, weaken
sign	—	trace, hint, signal, indication
slay	—	kill, murder, slaughter, butcher
smite	—	cuff, strike, defeat
steer	—	direct, pilot, guide
subject	—	theme, topic
suspend	—	delay, defer, hang
system	—	organization, method, cosmos
taboo	—	prohibited, banned
tally	—	account, score; register, count, enumerate
taste	—	savour, flavour, experience; appreciation, judgement
tear	—	rend, rip, split, lacerate
think	—	imagine, reflect, muse, recall, devise, consider
trap	—	snare, ambush
uniform	—	constant, undiversified, regular
unity	—	concert, harmony
variation	—	deviation, difference
venomous	—	malignant, virulent
vivid	—	bright, intense, clear, vigorous
walk	—	stride, stroll, saunter, perambulate
wane	—	diminish, decline, sink, decay
warp	—	distort, pervert
whole	—	undivided, integral, complete, intact, sound
yield	—	submit, concede, produce
zealous	—	eager, earnest, fervid, passionate, warm

DISTINCTIVE ADJECTIVES

Word	Adjective	Word	Adjective
air	pneumatic	matrimony	conjugal
ass	asinine	milk	lacteal
author	authorial	money	monetary
barber	tonsorial	moon	lunar
belly	alvine	morning	matinal
brain	cerebral	mother	maternal
cattle	bovine	night	nocturnal
coins	numismatic	nose	nasal
colour	chromatic	old age	senile
country	rustic, rural	parish	parochial
crow	corvine	pig	porcine
day	diurnal	river	fluvial
duke	ducal	sea	marine, maritime
earth	terrestrial	servant	menial
father	paternal	sheep	ovine
fish	piscine	ships, navy	naval
flood	diluvial	sight	optical, visual
fox	vulpine	sister	sororal
goat	caprine	smelling	olfactory
goose	anserine	son, daughter	filial
gums	gingival	sound	acoustic
hair	crinal	spring	vernal
hearing	auditory	stars	stellar
heart	cardiac	sun	solar
heaven	celestial	tailor	sartorial
horsemanship	equestrian	tears	lachrymal
infant	infantile	throat	guttural
kitchen	culinary	tin	stannic
land	praedial	town	urban
lion	leonine	uncle	avuncular
lips	labial	wife	uxorial
love	erotic	winter	brumal
lungs	pulmonary	wolf	lupine

SOUNDS MADE BY ANIMALS

apes	gibber	horses	neigh, whinny
asses	bray	hounds	bay
bears	growl	hyenas	scream
bees	hum	lions	roar
beetles	drone	mice	squeak
bulls	bellow	monkeys	chatter
cats	mew, purr	owls	hoot, screech
cocks	crow	parrots	screech
cows	moo, low	pigeons	coo
crickets	chirp	pigs	grunt
crows	caw	rabbits	squeal
dogs	bark	ravens	caw
doves	coo	robins	chirp
ducks	quack	rooks	caw
eagles	scream	seagulls	scream
elephants	trumpet	serpents	hiss
frogs	croak	sheep	bleat
geese	cackle	snakes	hiss
grasshoppers	chirr	turkeys	gobble
hens	cackle	wolves	howl

SOUNDS MADE BY THINGS

aeroplanes	zoom	horns	toot
arrows	whiz	horses' hoofs	clatter
bells	chime, tinkle	paper	crinkle
brakes	screech	silks	rustle
brooks	babble	steam	hisses
chains	clank	telephones	buzz, ring
clocks	tick	thunders	rumble
coins	jingle	waters	gurgle, lap, splash
corks	pop	whips	crack
fires	crackle	whistles	hoot
hammers	clang	winds	howl
hinges	creak	wings	whir

WORDS COMMONLY MIS-SPELT

abbreviation
abscess
abyss
adieu
adjacent
advice (*n.*)
advise (*v.*)
aisle
alms
altar
alter
altogether
amateur
antarctic
apparatus
appendix
arctic
asthma
athlete
atmosphere
audible
auxiliary
aviator
avoirdupois

bailiff
bankrupt
battalion
bayonet
bazaar
belfry
benefiting
besiege
biscuit
borough
bouquet
brief
buffet
bulletin
buoyant

bureau
business

calibre
camouflage
cashier
catarrh
catechism
ceiling
cemetery
centre
chalice
champagne
chaos
character
chasm
chassis
chauffeur
choir
chronic
column
committee
conceit
condemn
connoisseur
copse
coroner
corps
corpse
council
counsel
coupon

dairy
debris
debt
decease
deceive
dependant
dependent

depot
design
development
diaphragm
diarrhoea
diary
digestible
diphtheria
diphthong
discern
disease
dough
dungeon
dyeing
dying
dysentery

earnest
eccentric
eclipse
ecstasy
eczema
edible
ellipse
embalm
embarrass
embezzle
encyclopaedia
enthusiasm
envelope
eruption
etiquette
extinct

fashion
fatigue
favour
favourite
fibre
focusing

forcible
foreign
freight
fulfil

gaiety
galloping
gaol
gauge
geology
gnat
gnaw
goal
grieve
grotesque
guitar

haemorrhage
handkerchief
harass
hearse
heifer
height
heinous
hiccup
hippopotamus
hoeing
honorary
honour
humour
hydraulic
hygiene
hymn

icicle
impertinence
influenza
inseparable
install
instalment

16

instinct
irruption
islet

jealousy
judgement

kernel
khaki
kiln
knuckle

ladle
lair
laughter
laundry
leisure
lettuce
liar
library
licence *(n.)*
license *(v.)*
lieutenant
lighting
loquacious
luggage
luscious
lyre

malicious
manifestos
manoeuvre
martial
martyr
matinee
mechanic
medicine
mediterranean
memorandum
mileage
mischief

mischievous
mortgage
mosque
mosquito
mottoes
moustache
muscles
myrrh

neigh
neighbour
niece
ninety
noticeable

occurrence
oculist
operator
opponent
opportunity
overwhelm

pageant
paralysis
pavilion
permanence
persecutor
pharmacy
phlegm
photographer
photos
physician
plaque
plateau
plough
plumber
pneumonia
practice *(n.)*
practise *(v.)*
preliminary
principal

principle
privilege
psalm
psalter
psychology
psychiatrist
pursue

quay
queue

radius
realm
rebellion
receipt
receive
recipe
recommend
refrigerator
reign
rein
relieve
reminisce
rendezvous
reservoir
resign
rheumatism
rhythm
rogue

sabre
sanctify
sceptre
schism
scythe
seize
separate
sepulchre
siege
sieve
sign

skein
solemn
soliloquy
sombre
sorcery
sovereign
spasm
subpoena
subtle
suite
surety
surgeon
surveyor
sustenance
symmetry
synonym
syringe

tango
tariff
tarpaulin
technical
teetotaller
theatre
their
thigh
thorough
tincture
tomatoes
tongues
tough
tragedy
trophy
trousers
tuberculosis
typhoid

umbrella
unique
until
usury

veil	viscount	wharf	yoke
vein	visible	wholly	yolk
vicious		wilful	
victuals	weight	woollen	zephyr
villain	weird	wrestle	zinc

B. Use and Meaning of Words

SPECIAL TERMS

People

Achilles heel. The weak spot in the character of a person or nation.
April Gentleman. A newly married man.
Big-wig. A person with authority.
Cockney. A Londoner.
Curmudgeon. A greedy, miserly person.
Fairer sex, The. Women.
Fifth column. Traitors.
God's image. The human body.
Good Samaritan. A charitable and helpful friend to those in need.
Gotham, Wise men of. Fools.
Greenhorn. An inexperienced person.
Hercules' choice. Immortality.
Hobson's choice. No choice.
Ivan Ivanovitch. A Russian.
Jack Tar. A seaman.
Jeremiah. A doleful prophet.
John Bull. An Englishman.
Jonah. A person who brings bad luck.
Judas. A traitor.
Lazarus. A beggar.
Limb of the law. A policeman.
Man Friday. A faithful and willing attendant.
Man of letters. An author or scholar.
Sterner sex, The. Men.

Animals and Plants

American leopard. The jaguar.
Arabian bird. The phoenix.
Bird of Jove. The eagle.
Bird of Juno. The peacock.
Bird of Night. The owl.
Bird of Peace. The dove.
Indian corn. Maize.

King of beasts.   The lion.
King of the forest.   The oak.
King of the jungle.   The lion.
Lent lily.   The daffodil.

Places

Alhambra, The.   The citadel and palace built by the Moorish kings at Granada, Spain.
Bedlam.   A lunatic asylum.
Bodleian Library.   The excellent library at Oxford.
Bottomless Pit, The.   Hell.
Bride of the Sea.   Venice.
Celestial Empire.   China
Citadel of Athens, The.   The Acropolis.
Colosseum.   The amphitheatre in Rome.
Dark Continent, The.   Africa.
El Dorado.   A place where a person can become rich easily (City of Gold).
Eternal City, The.   Rome.
Fleet Street.   The center of journalism in England.
Garden of Europe.   Italy.
God's acre.   A burial ground.
Herring Pond, The.   The Atlantic Ocean.
House of correction.   A prison.
King of Waters.   The Amazon River.
King's House. Official Residence of the Govenor General of Jamaica
Kraal.   A South African native village.
Lamp of Heaven, The.   The moon.
Land o' the Leal.   Heaven.
Levant.   The eastern shore of the Mediterranean Sea.
Number 10, Downing Street.   The official residence of the British Prime Minister.
Old lady of Threadneedle Street, The.   The Bank of England.
Pillars of Hercules, The.   Gibraltar and Mount Hacho, two massive rocks on opposite sides at the entrance to the Mediterranean Sea.
River of Silver.   Rio de la Plata.
Silver Streak, The.   The English Channel.
Vale Royal.   The Official Residence of the Prime Minister of Jamaica.
Vatican, The.   The official residence of the Pope in Rome.
Wall Street.   The American stock market.
White House, The.   The official residence of the President of the United States of America.

Objects & Concepts

Adam's Ale.   Water.

Ashes, The.   Symbolic prize in cricket matches between England and Australia.

Black art.   Witchcraft, voodoo, obeah.

Black diamond.   Coal.

Black gold.   Oil.

Black Maria.   A prison van.

Calico.   A cotton cloth.

Cambric.   A fine linen cloth.

Fourth Estate, The.   The press.

Gentle craft, The.   Shoe-making.

Indian file.   A single file, with one person walking behind another.

Iron Horse.   A train.

King of metals.   Gold.

Ocean-greyhound.   A swift ship.

Olive branch, The.   A symbol of peace.

Paternoster.   The Lord's Prayer.

Scotland Yard.   The London Criminal Investigation Department.

Sheep's eyes, Make.   To look lovingly.

Sinews of war.   Money.

Tripos.   The honours examination at Cambridge University.

Universal Arithmetic, The.   Algebra.

White fuel.   Water power.

White Plague.   Tuberculosis.

Zephyr.   A soft, gentle wind.

OCCUPATIONS

Acrobat.   One who performs gymnastic feats.

Admiral.   The commander of a naval or merchant fleet.

Almoner.   A medical welfare officer who gives relief to the poor.

Anthropologist.   One who studies the evolution of mankind.

Archaeologist.   One who studies prehistoric remains.

Architect.   One who plans, designs and supervises the erection of buildings.

Astrologer.   One who predicts the future by the stars.

Astronomer.   One who studies the stars as a science.

Auctioneer.   One who conducts the sale of articles at auctions.

Auditor.   One who examines accounts.

Author.   One who writes books.

Aviator.   One who operates the flying controls of an aeroplane.

Brazier. One who works only in brass.
Bursar. One who manages the financial affairs of an institution.

Cartographer. One who draws maps.
Chandler. One who deals in candles.
Chauffeur. One who is employed to drive a motor car.
Chiropodist. One skilled in the treatment of feet.
Colporteur. One who peddles religious books.
Compositor. One who sets printing type.
Composer. One who composes musical pieces (original work).
Confectioner. One who sells a variety of sweets.
Cooper. One who makes casks and tubs.
Croupier. One who collects the bets and pays the winners at a gaming-table.
Curator. One who is in charge of a museum.
Cutler. One who makes or sells cutting instruments.

Dermatologist. One skilled in treating skin diseases.
Draughtsman. One who draws plans for structures.

Editor. One who prepares materials for publication or broadcast.
Ethnologist. One proficient in the science of races, their relations to one another and their characteristics.

Financier. One skilled in managing public money.
Fishmonger. One who deals in fish.
Florist. One who deals in flowers.
Funambulist. One skilled in walking on ropes.
Furrier. One who deals or works in furs.

Geologist. One who studies rocks and soils.
Glazier. One who fits glass in windows.
Grazier. One who breeds cattle for the market.

Haberdasher. One who sells a variety of clothing material.
Herbalist. One who grows or sells herbs for medical use.
Higgler. An itinerant trader of small articles.

Invigilator. One who watches over an examination.
Ironmonger. One who deals in hardware.

Janitor. One who takes care of a building.

Jockey.   One who rides professionally in horse races.
Journalist.   One who writes for a newspaper.

Lapidary.   One skilled in cutting precious stones.
Lexicographer.   One who compiles a dictionary.
Librarian.   One who is in charge of a library.

Masseur.   One who treats ailments by massaging the muscles.
Milliner.   One who make and sells hats.
Model.   One employed to wear garments for the benefit of customers.

Novelist.   One who writes novels.

Obstetrician.   A physician who attends to women at childbirth.
Ophthalmologist.   One who treats diseases of the eye.
Optician.   One who tests eyesight and prescribes and sells spectacles.

Pawnbroker.   One who lends money, keeping goods as security.
Pharmacist.   One who prepares and sells medicines and drugs.
Physician.   One who attends to the sick and prescribes medicine.
Psychiatrist.   One who treats mental illness.
Psychologist.   One who studies the workings of the human mind.
Purser.   One who is in charge of the stores and accounts on a ship.

Receptionist.   One who receives clients or visitors in an office.

Sculptor.   One who carves in stone, wood, metal.
Stationer.   One who sells paper, ink, pens and other writing materials.
Stenographer.   One skilled in writing shorthand.
Stevedore.   One who loads and unloads ships.
Surgeon.   One who treats ailments by performing operations.

Tanner.   One who makes leather from raw hide.
Taxidermist.   One who preserves and stuffs the skins of animals.
Teller.   One who receives and pays money at a bank.
Turnkey.   One who keeps the keys in a prison.

Undertaker.   One who manages funerals.
Upholsterer.   One who makes, repairs and sells cushions and seat covers.

Veterinarian.   One skilled in treating diseases of animals.

COLLECTIVE NOUNS

Anthology.   A choice collection of poems.
Army.   A large body of soldiers.
Audience.   An assembly of listeners.

Board.   A group of directors or administrators.
Bouquet.   A bunch of flowers.
Brood.   A number of young birds hatched at the same time.

Carillon.   A set of bells used as a musical instrument.
Catch.   An amount of fish caught.
Choir.   A group of singers, especially one belonging to a church.
Clump.   A group of trees.
Congregation.   A group of people attending a particular church.
Constellation.   A group of stars.
Convoy.   A number of ships or vehicles travelling under escort.
Cortège.   A funeral procession.
Crowd.   A large number of people pressed closely together.

Duet.   A pair of performers.

Fleet.   A number of ships, aircraft or motor cars.
Flight.   A number of birds or insects flying together.
Flock.   A number of animals, such as sheep and birds.
Forest.   A large extent of trees.

Gaggle.   A number of geese.
Galaxy.   A band of stars.
Group.   A number of persons or things standing or classed together.
Grove.   A small wood or group of trees.

Hand.   A fixed quantity of various commodities, e.g. a bundle of tobacco leaves.
Herbarium.   A collection of preserved plants.
Herd.   A number of animals, especially large ones such as cattle.
Hive.   A multitude of bees.

Leap.   A number of leopards.
Library.   A collection of books.
Litter.   A number of puppies, kittens, piglets, born at one birth.

Mob.   A group of disorderly people.

Pack.   A number of wolves, hounds or grouse.
Pride.   A group of lions.

School.   A number of whales or fish.
Sheaf.   A bundle of papers, arrows, corn-stalks.
Spectators.   A group of people looking on at a show or game.
Suite.   A set of matching furniture, rooms.
Swarm.   A large number of bees, locusts.

Tribe.   A group of persons of the same race.
Troop.   An assembly of persons or animals.
Troupe.   A group of entertainers.
Truss.   A bundle of hay.
Tuft.   A bunch of threads, grass, feathers.

WORDS RELATING TO MARRIAGE

Alimony.   Allowance paid by a person to his/her ex-spouse ordered by the court after a legal separation.
Banns.   Notice of intended marriage.
Betrothed.   Engaged to be married.
Bigamist.   One who marries a second husband or wife while still legally married to the first.
Celibate.   One who is bound or resolved not to marry usually because of a religious vow. Or one who is abstaining from sexual relations.
Divorce.   Legal dissolution of marriage.
Elope.   To run away secretly to get married.
Fiance, Fiancee.   One's betrothed.
Misogamist.   One who hates marriage.
Monogamist.   One who has only one wife or husband at a time.
Polygamist.   One who has more than one wife or husband at a time.
Trousseau.   Clothes and linen gathered by a bride in preparation for marriage.
Widow.   A woman whose husband is dead.
Widower.   A man whose wife is dead.

WORDS RELATING TO RELIGION

Acolyte.   One who assists with the performance of religious rites in the church.

Agnostic.   One who believes that nothing can be known about God beyond tangible phenomena.

Aisle.   A passage between the rows of seats in a church.

Anthem.   A composition for a church choir.

Apostate.   One who abandons his religious vows or principles.

Archdeacon.   A clergyman ranking immediately below a bishop.

Atheist.   One who does not believe in the existence of God.

Bigot.   One obstinately devoted to a particular creed.

Blaspheme.   Talk irreverently about God or religion.

Cassock.   A long, loose gown worn by the clergy and choristers.

Cathedral.   The principal church in the diocese.

Celebrant.   Officiating priest, especially at the Holy Communion.

Censer.   A vessel in which incense is burned.

Chalice.   The cup used in the Eucharist.

Chancel.   The eastern part of a church.

Chapel.   Part of a church or institution with an altar of its own for private worship.

Chaplain.   A clergyman assigned to a private chapel, a regiment, a warship, a prison or an institution.

Chorister.   One who sings in a choir.

Clergy.   All persons ordained for religious work.

Crosier.   The pastoral staff of a bishop or abbot.

Crypt.   A chapel or vault beneath a church usually used as a burial-place.

Diocese.   The district under the jurisdiction of a bishop.

Encyclical.   A letter from the Pope to all Roman Catholics.

Eucharist.   A ceremony in which bread (symbolic of Christ's body) and wine (symbolic of Christ's blood) are consumed as a means of honouring Christ's last meal before His curcifixion.

Evensong.   Evening prayer.

Font.   A receptacle for baptismal water.

Heresy.   An opinion contrary to the conventional belief.

Laity.   The people who are not the clergy.

Lectern.   A reading-desk in church from where the scriptures are read.

Manse.   The residence of a clergyman.
Matins.   Morning prayer in the Church of England.
Missionary.   One who goes on religious missions.
Mitre.   A tall cap worn by bishops and abbots.
Monotheist.   One who believes in one god.

Nave.   The central part of a church.

Offertory.   The money collected at a church service.
Ordination.   The ceremony at which a person is admitted to the Christian ministry.

Polytheist.   One who believes in many gods.
Proselyte.   One who is converted from one religion to another.
Pulpit.   The raised platform from which a preacher delivers his sermon.

Repentance.   The act of regretting one's actions.
Rosary.   A string of beads used by Roman Catholics in prayers.

Sexton.   One who looks after a church building and attends to the clergyman.
Stipend.   The salary of a clergyman.
Surplice.   A loose, white-linen vestment with full sleeves worn over the cassock by the clergy.
Synod.   An ecclesiastical council.

Vespers.   Evening service.
Vestment.   The garment of the clergy and choristers.
Vestry.   A room attached to a church for keeping vestments and holding meetings.

Wafer.   A thin, round bread used in the Eucharist.

WORDS RELATING TO DEATH

Asphyxia.   Fainting or death caused by a lack of oxygen.
Autopsy.   An examination of a dead body.

Bier.   A carriage for conveying the dead to the grave.

Carcass.   The dead body of an animal.
Carrion.   The dead and decomposing body of an animal.
Catacombs.   Underground galleries with recesses for tombs.

Catafalque. A decorated stage for a coffin used during funeral ceremonies; an open hearse.

Cemetery. A place where dead bodies are buried.

Cenotaph. A monument to the dead who are buried elsewhere.

Corpse. The body of a dead human being.

Cremation. Disposal of a corpse by burning.

Cryonics. The practice of freezing a body with the intention of reviving it years later.

Electrocuted. Killed by electricity.

Embalm. To preserve a corpse from decay

Epitaph. An inscription on a tomb.

Euthanasia. Painless killing of someone with an incurable disease.

Executioner. One who puts condemned persons to death.

Exequies. Funeral rites.

Exhume. To dig up a corpse from its grave.

Fratricide. Murder of one's brother.

Hearse. A vehicle for transporting dead bodies to the cemetery.

Homicide. Killing of a human being.

Infanticide. Murder of a baby or a very young child.

Intestate. To die without making a will.

Legacy. Money or property left to someone by will.

Matricide. Murder of one's mother.

Mausoleum. A magnificent tomb.

Morgue. A place where bodies of persons are laid out for identification.

Mortuary. A place where dead bodies are temporarily kept.

Obituary. A notice of death in the newspaper; a brief biography of a deceased person.

Parricide. Murder of one's parent or near relative.

Patricide. Murder of one's father.

Posthumous. Occurring after death.

Post-mortem. Medical examination of a dead body.

Pyre. A pile of combustible material on which a dead body is burned.

Regicide. Murder of a king.

Requiem.   Special mass for the soul of the dead.

Shroud.   The garment for the dead.
Sororicide.   Murder of one's sister.
Suicide.   Killing of oneself.

INSTRUMENTS AND THEIR USES

Ammeter.   An instrument for measuring electric current.
Anemometer.   An instrument for measuring the force of wind.

Barometer.   An instrument for measuring the atmospheric pressure.
Binoculars.   An instrument for both eyes which makes distant objects appear nearer.

Camera.   An instrument for taking photographs.
Compass.   An instrument for finding directions.

Gyrograph.   An instrument for recording revolutions.

Hodometer.   An instrument for measuring distance travelled by a wheeled vehicle.

Lithoscope.   An instrument for distinguishing precious stones.

Manometer.   An instrument for measuring the pressure of gases.
Metronome.   An instrument for marking time in music.
Micrometer.   An instrument for measuring minute objects or distances.
Microphone.   An instrument for increasing the volume of sound.
Microscope.   An instrument for magnifying small objects.

Periscope.   An instrument that enables an observer in a submarine or trench to see objects above the surface.

Seismograph.   An instrument that registers earthquakes.
Speedometer.   An instrument for measuring the speed of a vehicle.

Telephone.   An instrument for transmitting sound to a distance.
Telescope.   An instrument for making distant objects appear nearer.
Thermometer.   An instrument for measuring temperature.

WORDS RELATING TO NATURE STUDY

Absorption.   The process by which plants absorb mineral salts through their roots.

Alluvium.   Soil transported and deposited by rivers and floods.

Amphibious.   Living both on land and in water.

Annual.   A plant that lasts only one year or season.

Antennae.   The feelers of an insect.

Antler.   A branch of a stag's horn.

Assimilation.   The process by which plants produce food.

Biennial.   A plant that lasts for two years.

Bulb.   Underground shoot with thick stem and leaves.

Chlorophyll.   The colouring matter in the green parts of plants.

Chrysalis.   The transition stage between larva and adult in the development of an insect.

Core.   The innermost part of a fruit.

Cotyledon.   The seed leaf in the embryo of a plant.

Deciduous.   Plants which shed their leaves annually.

Dibble.   An instrument to make holes in the ground for seeds.

Dicotyledons.   Plants with two seed leaves.

Embryo.   Organism of animal before birth or hatching.

Fauna.   The animals found in a certain region.

Fertilisation.   Union of two sex cells to form a zygote which develops into a new plant or animal.

Flax.   Fibres from a plant from which linen is woven.

Forage.   Food for horses and cattle.

Fossil.   The hardened remains of a plant or animal preserved in rock.

Germination.   Growth of a plant from seed.

Gregarious.   Living in flocks or herds.

Hibernation.   The dormant or resting state in which some animals pass the winter.

Humus.   Decayed vegetable matter in the soil.

Inflorescence.   The flower part of a plant.

Insecticide. A preparation used for killing insects.
Invertebrate. An animal without backbone.
Irrigate. To supply land with water by means of canals.

Kernel. The edible part of a nut.

Mandible. The lower jaw in vertebrates; the upper or lower part of a bird's beak.
Marsupial. An animal which carries its young in a pouch.
Monocotyledons. Plants with one seed leaf.
Mutton. The flesh of sheep as food.

Naturalist. One who studies plant and animal life.

Offal. The internal organs of an animal killed for food.
Ore. Rock from which mineral can be extracted.

Parasite. An animal or plant living on another.
Perennial. A plant that lives for many years.
Plumule. The embryo shoot in a seed.
Pollination. The transference of pollen from stamen to stigma.

Quadruped. A four-footed animal.

Radicle. The part of a plant embryo that develops into the primary root.
Respiration. Breathing, the process of taking in oxygen and giving out carbon dioxide.
Rhizome. An underground stem.
Rodent. A gnawing animal such as a squirrel.
Ruminant. An animal that chews the cud.

Slough. A dead skin cast off by a living animal.
Spoor. The track or scent of a hunted animal.
Stipules. Two leaf-like projections at the base of a leaf stalk.
Stomata. Openings on the green parts of a plant for breathing.

Tendril. A slender part of a plant which attaches itself to another body for support.
Transpiration. Passage of water vapour from inside a plant to the atmosphere through its leaves.

Venison.   The flesh of deer as food.
Vertebrate.   An animal with a spinal column.

WORDS RELATING TO GOVERNMENT

Abdication.   The voluntary giving up of the throne by a king or queen.
Aristocracy.   Government by the nobility.
Autocracy.   Government by a sovereign with unlimited authority.
Autonomy.   The right of self-government.

Ballot.   Secret voting.
Bureaucracy.   Government administered by non-elective officials.

Cabinet.   A select body of ministers chosen by the head of the
   government to be in charge of various government departments.
Campaign.   The seeking of votes by a politician in an election.
Coalition.   A temporary union of political parties.
Communism.   Dictatorship government by a party carried out in the
   name of the people.
Consort.   The wife or husband of a reigning monarch.
Constituency.   A body of voters that is represented in government.
Coup d'etat.   A violent or unconstitutional take-over of government.

Democracy.   Government which respects the basic rights of its citizens.
Despotocracy.   Government by one having absolute power.
Détente.   The easing of strained relationship between two countries.
Dynasty.   A succession of rulers from one family.

Egalitarianism.   Government ruling on the principle of equality for all
   citizens.
Election.   Choosing of candidates for office by vote.
Episcopacy.   Government by bishops.

Franchise.   The right to vote at elections.

Hierarchy.   Levels of authority in government.

Impeachment.   The accusation and prosecution for crime against the state.
Interregnum.   The period between the end of a reign and the beginning
   of the next.

Kakistocracy.   Government by the worst citizens.

Manifesto.   A public declaration of policy by a candidate, political party or ruler.

Monarchy.   Government by a sovereign ruler.

Oligarchy.   Government by a small group of people.

Plutocracy.   Government by the wealthy.

Politics.   The science or art of government.

Referendum.   The referring of a political question to a direct vote of the electorate.

Revolution.   Complete change in government by force.

Socialism.   A political and economic theory that advocates state ownership of the means of production and equal distribution of wealth.

Theocracy.   Government by a priestly class.

WORDS RELATING TO ARTS AND SCIENCES

Agriculture.   The art of cultivating the soil.
Agronomics.   The science of land management.
Anatomy.   The science of the human structure.
Anthropology.   The science of man.
Archaeology.   The study of human antiquities.
Astrology.   The art of interpreting the influence of stars on human affairs.
Astronomy.   The science of the heavenly bodies.

Biology.   The science of physical life.
Botany.   The science of plants.

Calligraphy.   The art of beautiful handwriting.
Cartography.   The art of map-making.
Cloning. Asexually producing an organism or cell from an ancestor to which it is genetically identical.

Ecology. The study of living organisms in relation to the environment.

Ethnology. The science which deals with the varieties of human race.
Etymology. The science of the origin and meaning of words.

Genealogy. The study of family history and descent.
Geology. The science of the earth's crust.

Horticulture. The art of garden cultivation.
Hydrology. The science of the properties of water.

Jurisprudence. The science of the law.

Limnology. The study of lakes or pond life.

Mathematics. The science of magnitude and number.
Mensuration. The science of measuring length, area and volume.
Metallurgy. The art of working metals.

Numismatics. The study of coins and medals.

Oology. The study of birds' eggs.
Ornithology. The study of birds.
Orology. The study of mountains.

Palaeography. The study of ancient writings.
Phiology. The science of language.
Physiognomy. The art of judging character from appearance.
Physiology. The science of vital functions in animals and plants.

Seismology. The science of earthquakes.
Surveying. The art of measuring land.

Taxidermy. The art of preserving skins of dead animals.
Technology. The science of the industrial arts.

Zoology. The science of animal life.

WORDS RELATING TO LAW

Acquittal. Discharge from prosecution for an offence tried in court.
Adjourn. To suspend proceedings in order to continue at a later date.

Affidavit.   A written statement on oath signed before a witness.
Alibi.   Plea that a person was elsewhere when a crime was committed.
Appeal.   To seek another judgement from a higher court.
Arraign.   To accuse, put to trial.
Attest.   To bear witness to.
Attorney.   A solicitor; one legally authorized to act for another.

Bail.   Security given to ensure that a person appears for trial.

Codicil.   A supplement to a will.
Contempt of court.   An offence against the dignity of a court.
Contest.   To defend an issue in court.

Decree nisi.   An order for divorce that will become absolute after a certain period.
Defendant.   One against whom a claim or charge is brought.
Due process.   The various stages in the administration of the law.

Evidence.   Information presented in court to establish a fact.
Executor.   A person named by a deceased to carry out the provisions of his will.

Habeas corpus.   A writ requiring a person to be brought before a court.

Indemnify.   To protect against possible loss; to compensate for actual loss.

Jury.   A body of persons sworn to render a verdict to a court.

Legacy.   A gift of property by will.
Lessee.   One to whom a lease is granted.
Lessor.   One who grants a lease.
Libel.   A published statement that damages a person's reputation.

Magistrate.   A civil officer charged with the administration of the law.

Plaintiff.   A person who brings suit in a court.

Slander.   Defamation in transient form.
Sue.   To institute proceedings against somebody in court.

Testimony.   Oral evidence of a witness in court.

Verdict.   Decision reached by a jury.

LITERARY WORDS

Acrostic. A poem in which the first letter, or the first and last letters, of each line form a word or sentence.

Alliteration.   The repetition of an initial letter in successive words.

Anagram.   Word or words formed by rearranging the letters in a given word.

Autobiography.   An account of a person's life written by himself.

Bibliography.   A descriptive list of books on a particular subject or by a particular author.

Biography.   An account of the life of a person.

Blank verse.   An unrhymed verse.

Caption.   The heading of an article or chapter; the words accompanying an illustration or photograph.

Comedy.   A humorous play with a happy ending.

Copyright.   The exclusive right of an author or composer to reproduce his original work.

Dirge.   A funeral song or poem.

Dramatist.   One who writes plays.

Elegy.   A song or poem of lamentation, especially for the dead.

Epitome.   A summary of a book.

Erratum.   An error in printing or writing.

Eulogy.   A speech or writing in praise of a person.

Euphemism.   A mild word or phrase that is substituted for one that may be considered to be offensive.

Excerpt.   An extract from a book.

Expurgate.   To purify by removing offensive matter from a book.

Extant.   Still in existence (of documents or books).

Facsimile.   An exact copy of a picture, handwriting or printing.

Frontispiece.   A picture facing the title page of a book.

Glossary.   A list and explanations of technical or obsolete words.

Hackneyed.   Language that is too commonly used.

Harangue.   A loud or vehement speech to a large audience intended to excite passions.

Hyperbole.   Intentional exaggeration of a particular situation in order to produce an effect.

Impromptu.   Given without preparation (of a speech or performance).

Memoirs.   An autobiographical account of one's experiences.

Memorandum.   A note to help the memory.

Oxymoron.   Two words or terms that seem to be contrasting in meaning put together.

Peroration.   The conclusion of a speech.

Plagiarism.   Taking of somebody else's writing and passing it off as one's own.

Playwright.   One who writes plays.

Prologue.   An introductory speech at the beginning of a play.

Soliloquy.   Talking to oneself.

Tragedy.   A play with a lofty theme and sad ending.

Vernacular.   The native language of a country.

Watermark.   A distinguishing mark in paper visible when it is held against the light.

SLANG WORDS

Jamaica

A buguyaga. A slovenly, clumsy person.

A ginal. A tricky person.

Aback. In the past.

A it mek.   That is the reason.

A nuh nutten.   It's no big deal.

Back-answer.   Retort sharply, reply.

Back weh.   Move away.

Bangarang.   Good for nothing.

Bashy.   Fabulous; Nice.

Boots.   Condoms.

Cha Cha Bwoy.   A man dressed in the latest fashions.
Cris.   Pretty, Fine.
Cuss blue light.   Use indecent language.
Cut ten.   Sit with legs crossed.

Dem was a labrish.   They were gossiping.
Don.   The most feared and respected man in the community.
Don't advantage mi.   Do not ill-treat me.
Dread.   A Rastafarian.
Dress yu self.   Move yourself.

Eh go so.   That's the way it goes.

Fandangle up the place.   Decorate the place excessively.
Fassy 'ole.   Someone who acts unfairly or unreasonably.
Fyah bun.   To emphatically denounce someone or something.

Gallis.   A promiscuous male.
Gree.   Agree.
Go si dung pon yu face.   Stop talking.

Hile.   Oil.
Him hackle mi.   He works me hard.
Him likkle but him tallawa.   He is small but he is strong.
Hottie hottie.   Young lady who is well dressed and attractive.

Idrin.   Friend.
Infahmah.   Informer; Snitch.

Jack Mandora mi no choose none.   This story is not aimed at you or anyone.
Jah.   God.
Jizzle.   Drizzle.

Kawz.   Cause.
Kibba.   Shut.
Kin puppa lick.   To somersault.

Lickie lickie.   Greedy.
Leggo.   Let go.

Marina.   Tank top.
Mo fyah.   More fire.

Moss. To hide something.

No mell me. Don't interfere with me.
Natty. Knotted; Dreadlocks.

Ooman. Woman.

Paypa. Paper.
Poco-poco. Fairly well (reply to the greeting "How are you?").
Pyaa-pyaa. Weak, inferior.

Rahtid. An exclamation of anger or surprise.
Ruff neck. Tough guy.
Runkus. A wild party or dance.

Samfie. A dishonest person.
Screechie. Jamaican dance move.
Sheg. To spoil.
Shotta. A person who is well respected.
Susu. To gossip.

Tandeh. Stay there.
Teggereg. An uncouth person, a troublemaker.
To fene. To faint, or feel discomfort.

Undred. Hundred.

War boat. Quarrelsome individual.
Wat a kas-kas. What a quarrel.
Winji. Weak.

Yu have age paper? Do you have your birth certificate?
Yush. An informal greeting.

Zeen. Okay.

Trinidad and Tobago

Catch yuhself. Take hold of yourself.
Cutting style. Showing off.

Doan gi me fatigue.   Do not ridicule me.
Doe make skylark.   Do not joke.
Doe mamaguy me man.   Do not make a fool of me.

Everything tun ole mas.   Everything became confused.

Foe-day-morning.   Just before sunrise.

Licks like bush.   Plenty licks.
Lime.   To idle.

Man, she cutting.   Man, she is looking well.
More guts than a breadfruit.   Bold face.

Now fuh now.   Right now.

Wee fute.   An exclamation of surprise.

Barbados

Bram.   A small dancing party.
Brass up.   Telling off or dressing down.
Bring down.   To cause unpleasantness.

Chinky.   Stingy, miserly.
Come lewwe fire one.   Let us have a drink.

Nick.   To throw dice.

Paipsey.   Of insipid or unattractive appearance.
Pooch.   Backside.
Pooma.   An old motor car.
Pump.   To get a free ride.

Razzy.   Shabby, down at heel.

Weed.   An expert.

Yam.   To eat greedily.

Guyana

Aise.   Ears.
Ah-deh.   "I'm tolerably well."

Bacalay.   Fuss.
Bassa-bassa.   Aggressive, fussy.
Bittle.   Food.
Bourriddee.   A glutton for anything – games, food, dancing, etc.

Cagas.   A certificate to get a job.
Cankawah.   An unpredictable person.
Caraboca.   Shut your mouth.
Cass-cass.   Careless, disorganized, jumbled.
Crake.   To rebuke petulantly.
Cramp.   Iced water.

Freck.   A small amount of money given in charity.

Gar bar.   Nonsense, unnecessary obstruction.

Hyse.   To lift oneself.

Kangalang.   A lawless, ignorant person.

La laaf.   To relax or lie lazily about.

Metcha-metcha.   Fancy trappings on a garment, etc.

Patchuma.   Undersized.
Piasse.   To show off.

Bahamas

Asue.   Collective savings plan by which Bahamians accumulate large sums of money to make special purchases or payments.

Benne.   Sesame seeds.

41

Camolly. A lump.
Chirren. Your offspring.

Duff. A boiled fruit filled dough.

Emp. Pour out.

Ferl. A thin continuous sheet of metal.

Hice. Hoist.

Jack. Friend.

Kaprang. An old bicycle.

Leg short. Too late.

Miss lady. Polite form of address for women.

Ogly. Ugly.

Palt. To throw stones at.

Shuttail. Naked.

Tote news. Gossip.

Upstairs house. A residence with more than one storey.

PROVERBS

A bad excuse is better than none.
A bad workman blames his tools.
A beggar can never be bankrupt.
A bird in hand is worth two in the bush.
A burnt child dreads fire.
A cat may look at a King.
A cheerful look makes a dish a feast.
A cheerful wife is the joy of life.
A drowning man will catch at a straw.

A fair exchange is no robbery.
A fault confessed is half redressed.
A fool and his money are soon parted.
A fool may give a wise man counsel.
A fool may make money, but it takes a wise man to spend it.
A friend in need is a friend indeed.
A friend to all is a friend to none.
A good name is better than riches.
A good wife makes a good husband.
A guilty conscience needs no accuser.
A hungry man is an angry man.
A little help is worth a lot of pity.
A man is as old as he feels; a woman is as old as she looks.
A man's house is his castle.
A miss is as good as a mile.
A penny saved is a penny gained.
A pound of care won't pay an ounce of debt.
A rolling stone gathers no moss.
A rose between two thorns.
A stitch in time saves nine.
A wise man changes his mind sometimes, a fool never.
A wonder lasts but nine days.
A word to the wise is enough.
Absence makes the heart grow fonder.
Action speaks louder than words.
After a storm comes a calm.
All covet, all lose.
All is not gold that glitters.
All work and no play makes Jack a dull boy.
All's fair in love and war.
Among the blind the one-eyed man is king.
An army marches on its stomach.
An idle brain is the devil's workshop.
An ounce of prevention is worth a pound of cure.
Any port in a storm.
As you make your bed, so you must lie on it.
As you sow, so you shall reap.
Avoid evil and it will avoid you.

Barking dogs seldom bite.
Be just before you are generous.

Beggars cannot be choosers.
Better be alone than in ill company.
Better do it than wish it done.
Better late than never.
Between the devil and the deep blue sea.
Birds of a feather flock together.
Blood is thicker than water.
Brevity is the soul of wit.
Bullies are generally cowards.
By others' faults wise men correct their own.

Catch not at the shadow and lose the substance.
Charity begins at home.
Civility costs nothing.
Curiosity killed a cat.
Cut your coat according to your cloth.

Dead men tell no tales.
Delays are dangerous.
Destiny leads the willing, but drags the unwilling.
Diligence is a great teacher.
Discretion is the better part of valour.
Do as I say, not as I do.
Do as you would be done by.
Do not count your chickens before they are hatched.
Do not cut off your nose to spite your face.
Do not put all your eggs in one basket.
Do not tell tales out of school.

Early to bed and early to rise makes a man healthy, wealthy and wise.
Easier said than done.
Easy come, easy go.
Eat to live, but do not live to eat.
Employment brings enjoyment.
Empty vessels make the most noise.
Enough is as good as a feast.
Enough is better than too much.
Every ass loves his own bray.
Every cloud has a silver lining.
Every dog has its day.
Every little helps.

Every man for himself and God for us all.
Every man must carry his own cross.
Every why has a wherefore.
Everyone can find fault, few can do better.
Everyone knows best where the shoe pinches.
Everyone thinks his own burden is the heaviest.
Everything comes to those who wait.
Example is better than precept.
Experience teaches wisdom.

Familiarity breeds contempt.
Fancy kills and fancy cures.
Fire is a good servant but a bad master.
First come, first served.
Flattery brings friends, truth enemies.
Flies are easier caught with honey than with vinegar.
Follow the river and you will find the sea.
Forewarned is forearmed.
Fortune favours the brave.

Gentle in manner, but resolute in action.
Give a dog a bad name and hang him.
Give everyone his due.
Give him an inch and he'll take a mile.
Give the devil his due.
God helps those who help themselves.
God never shuts one door but he opens another.
Good beginnings make good endings.
Good masters make good servants.
Grasp all, lose all.
Gratitude is the least of virtues, ingratitude the worst of vices.
Great haste makes great waste.
Great minds think alike.
Great profits, great risks.

Half a loaf is better than none.
Hasty climbers have sudden falls.
He is richest that has fewest wants.
He laughs best who laughs last.
He that knows little soon repents it.
He that knows nothing doubts nothing.

He that will eat the kernel must crack the nut.
He who ceases to pray ceases to prosper.
He who goes a-borrowing goes a-sorrowing.
He who likes borrowing dislikes paying.
Here today and gone tomorrow.
He's no man who cannot say "No".
His bark is worse than his bite.
Honesty is the best policy.
Hope is the last thing that we lose.

If a man deceives me once, shame on him; if twice, shame on me.
If at first you don't succeed, try, try, try again!
If the cap fits, wear it.
If the mountain will not come to Mohammed,
      Mohammed must go to the mountain.
If wishes were horses, beggars would ride.
Ill got, ill spent.
Ill news travels fast.
In for a penny, in for a pound.
It is a long lane that has no turning.
It is always time to do good.
It is an ill wind that blows nobody good.
It is easier to get money than to keep it.
It is easier to pull down than to build.
It is easy to be wise after the event.
It is never too late to mend.
It is no use crying over spilt milk.
It never rains but it pours.
It takes two to make a quarrel.

Jack of all trades, master of none.

Kill not the goose that lays the golden eggs.
Kill two birds with one stone.
Kind words are worth much and cost little.
Kindle not a fire you cannot extinguish.
Knowledge is power.

Lend only what you can afford to lose.
Let bygones be bygones.
Let sleeping dogs lie.

Like father, like son.
Like mother, like daughter.
Little boats must keep the shore, Larger boats may venture more.
Live and let live.
Look before you leap.
Love is blind.

Make every bargain clear and plain, that none may afterwards complain.
Make hay while the sun shines.
Make short the miles, with talk and smiles.
Man proposes, God disposes.
Manners maketh man.
Many hands make light work.
Many straws may bind an elephant.
Marry in haste, repent at leisure.
Men make houses, women make homes.
Money talks.
More haste, less speed.

Necessity is the mother of invention.
Neither wise men nor fools can work without tools.
Never cross the bridge until you come to it.
Never do things by halves.
Never hit a man when he's down.
Never look a gift-horse in the mouth.
Never put off until tomorrow what can be done today.
Never too old to learn.
New broom sweeps clean.
No gains without pains.
No man is without enemies.
No news is good news.
No rose without a thorn.
No smoke without fire.
None so blind as those who will not see.
None so deaf as those who will not hear.
Nothing succeeds like success.
Nothing ventured, nothing gained.

On a long journey even a straw is heavy.
Once bitten, twice shy.
One can live on a little, but not on nothing.

One cannot die twice.
One good turn deserves another.
One man's meat is another man's poison.
One may sooner fall than rise.
One swallow does not make a summer.
One Today is worth two Tomorrows.
Out of debt, out of danger.
Out of sight, out of mind.
Out of the frying pan into the fire.
Pardon all men, but never thyself.
Penny wise, pound foolish.
Practice makes perfect.
Practise what you preach.
Prevention is better than cure.
Pride goes before a fall.
Procrastination is the thief of time.
Punctuality is the soul of business.
Put not your trust in money; put your money in trust.
Put your own shoulder to the wheel.

Rashness is not valour.
Reckless youth makes rueful age.
Rome was not built in a day.
Rumour is a great traveller.

Saying is one thing; doing another.
Second thoughts are best.
Seeing is believing.
Set a thief to catch a thief.
Silence gives consent.
Six of one and half a dozen of the other.
Slow and steady wins the race.
Sometimes the best gain is to lose.
Sooner said than done.
Spare the rod and spoil the child.
Speak little but speak the truth.
Speak well of your friends, and of your enemies nothing.
Speaking without thinking is shooting without aim.
Speech is silver; silence is golden.
Spilt salt is never all gathered.
Still waters run deep.
Strike while the iron is hot.

Take care of the pence and the pounds will take care of themselves.
Talk of the devil and he'll appear.
That which is evil is soon learnt.
The best of friends must part.
The child is father of the man.
The darkest hour is before the dawn.
The early bird catches the worm.
The grass is greener on the other side of the fence.
The less people think, the more they talk.
The more the merrier.
The pot calls the kettle black.
The proof of the pudding is in the eating.
The receiver is as bad as the thief.
The road to hell is paved with good intentions.
The stone that lieth not in your way need not offend you.
The unexpected always happens.
The wish is father to the thought.
There are more foolish buyers than foolish sellers.
There are two sides to every question.
There could be no great ones if there were no little.
There is a "But" in everything.
There is a time for all things.
There is no true love without jealousy.
There's many a slip 'twixt the cup and the lip.
There's safety in numbers.
They who only seek for faults find nothing else.
Those who live in glass houses should not throw stones.
Those who make the best use of their time have none to spare.
Time and tide wait for no man.
Time cures more than the doctor.
Time is the best counsellor.
Tit for tat is fair play.
To be born with a silver spoon in the mouth.
To err is human; to forgive divine.
To kill two birds with one stone.
To know the disease is half the cure.
To look for a needle in a haystack.
To scare a bird is not the best way to catch it.
Too many cooks spoil the broth.
True love never grows old.
Trust but not too much.
Truth is stranger than fiction.

Turn over a new leaf.
Two is company, three's none.
Two wrongs do not make a right.

Undertake no more than you can perform.
Union is strength.

Virtue is its own reward.
Vows made in storms are forgotten in calms.

Wash your dirty linen at home.
Waste not, want not.
We can live without our friends, but not without our neighbours.
Well begun is half done.
What belongs to everybody belongs to nobody.
What can't be cured must be endured.
What is learnt in the cradle lasts to the tomb.
What is sauce for the goose is sauce for the gander.
What the eye does not admire the heart does not desire.
What the eye does not see the heart does not grieve over.
Whatever's worth doing at all is worth doing well.
When in Rome do as the Romans do.
When poverty comes in at the door, love flies out of the window.
Where there is nothing to lose, there is nothing to fear.
Where there is smoke there is fire.
Where there's a will there's a way.
While there is life there is hope.
Who chatters to you will chatter of you.
Whom the gods love die young.

You cannot have your cake and eat it too.
You cannot get blood out of a stone.
You cannot make a silk purse out of a sow's ear.
You cannot see the wood for the trees.
You cannot teach old dogs new tricks.
You may take a horse to the water, but you cannot make him drink.
You never know till you have tried.
Young men think old men fools; old men know young men to be so.
Youth lives on hope, old age on remembrance.

Zeal without knowledge is fire without light.

C. Vocabulary Development

PREFIXES

A prefix is a letter or group of letters added in front of a word which alters its meaning.

Prefix	Meaning	Examples
a-	away, on, up, out	arise, ashore, afloat
a-, ab-, abs-	away from	avert, abnormal, absent
ad- (a-, ac-, af-, ag-, al-, an-, ap-, ar-, as-, at-)	to	admire, achieve, accede, affix, aggregate, allot, annex, append, arrive, assign, attain
ambi-, amphi-	both	ambidexter, amphibian
ante-	before	antecedent, antedate
anti-	against	antidote, antipathy
arch-	first, chief	archetype, archbishop
auto-	self	autobiography, autograph
bene-	well	benefactor, benevolent
bi-, bis-, bin-	two, twice	biscuit, bilingual, binoculars
cata-, cath-	down, thoroughly	cataract, catholic
circum-	round about	circumference
con-, co-, com-, col-, cor-	with, together	connect, co-operate, combine, collaborate, correct
de-	down, away, from	descent, deduce, deflect
deca-	ten	decagon, decade
demi-	half	demigod
dia-	through	diameter, diagonal
dis-, di-	in two, asunder	dissyllable, differ
ec-, ex-	out of, from	ecstasy, exodus, exhume
epi-	on	epitaph
equi-	equal	equidistant, equivalent
eu-	well	eulogy, euphony
ex-	former	ex-soldier, ex-convict

Prefix	Meaning	Examples
extra-	beyond	extraordinary, extramural
fore-	before	foretell, foresight
hemi-	half	hemisphere
hepta-	seven	heptagon, heptarchy
hetero-	different	heterogeneous, heterodoxy
hexa-	six	hexagon, hexahedron
homo-	same	homogeneous, homonym
hyper-	beyond, above	hyperbole, hypertension
hypo-	under	hypogeal
in- (ig-, il-, im-, ir-)	not	informal, ignoble, illegible, immature, irregular
in- (il-, im-, ir- em-, en-)	into (used in verbs)	infuse, illustrate, import, irrigate, enrol, embrac
inter-	between	intervene, interval
intra-	within	intramural, intravenous
intro-	within	introduce, introspect
juxta-	near	juxtaposition
mal-, male-	bad	malefactor, malediction, malice, malcontent
meta-, met-	change	metamorphose, metonymy
mis-	wrong	mislead, misjudge
mono-	one	monarch, monocle
ne-, non-	not	negative, nonsense
ob- (o-, oc-, of-, op-, os-)	against, in the way of	obstacle, omit, occasion, offend, oppose, ostentation
omni-	all	omnipotent, omnipresent
para-, par-	beside, beyond	parallel, parable
pen-, pene-	almost	peninsula, peneplain
penta-	five	pentagon
per- (par-, pel-, pil-)	through, thoroughly	perfect, pardon, pellucid, pilgrim
peri-	around	perimeter

Prefix	Meaning	Examples
poly-	many	polygamy, polygon
post-	after	postdate, postscript
pre-	before	predecessor, predict
preter-	beyond	preternatural, preterhuman
pro-	forward, instead of	pronoun, project, propel
pro-	before	prologue, prophet
pseudo-	false	pseudonym
re-, red-, ren-	back, again, against, reversed	rediscover, retract, redeem, render
retro-	backwards	retrograde, retrospect
se-	without, aside, apart	secure, seduce, separate
semi-	half	semicircle, semifinal
sine-	without	sinecure
sub-	under	submarine, subordinate
super-	over, beyond	superhuman, supernatural
sur-	over	surmount
trans-	across	transport, transmit
tri-	three	triangle, tripod, triple
ultra-	beyond	ultra-modern, ultra-violet
vice-	in place of	viceroy, vice-president

SUFFIXES

A suffix is a letter or group of letters added at the end of a word which, like the prefix, alters its meaning.

Suffix	Meaning	Examples
-able, -ible, -uble	capable of being	believable, incredible, soluble
-age	state	marriage, bondage
-ain, -an	one connected	chaplain, Georgian
-al	belonging to	constitutional, national
-ance, -ence	quality, state	tolerance, penitence

Suffix	Meaning	Examples
-ant, -ent	one who	servant, patient
-ate	to make	animate, navigate
-ation	act of	dedication, education
-cy	practice of	democracy
-dom	state of, power	freedom, kingdom
-en	to make	moisten, darken
-er	one who does	writer, singer
-fold	number	threefold, manifold
-ful	full of	respectful, thoughtful
-hood	state of	brotherhood, manhood
-ic	belonging to	fantastic, gigantic
-ify	to make	gratify, falsify
-ion	act of	decision, conclusion
-ism	state	fascism, plagiarism
-ist	one who practices	communist, artist
-less	lacking	useless, tasteless
-logy	study of, discourse	geology, eulogy
-ness	state	smoothness, hardness
-or	one who does	tailor, sailor
-ory	belonging to, place where	compulsory, dormitory
-ous	full of	mountainous, religious
-ry	action, quality, condition, occupation	sorcery, slavery, dentistry
-ship	state of	partnership, friendship
-ty	state, quality	dignity, fidelity
-ward	direction	westward, homeward
-y	full of, quality of	smoky, bony

SIMILES

as ageless as the sun
as agile as a monkey
as alike as two peas
as alone as Crusoe

as bald as a coot
as beautiful as the rainbow
as big as an elephant

as bitter as gall
as black as coal
as bold as a lion
as brown as berry

as chaste as a lily
as cheap as dirt
as clear as daylight

as cold as a corpse
as constant as the sun
as cool as a cucumber
as crafty as a fox

as dark as a dungeon
as desolate as a tomb
as distant as the horizon
as dry as dust

as eager as a bridegroom
as easy as winking
as eloquent as Cicero

as faithful as a dog
as far apart as the poles
as fast as light
as fit as a fiddle
as fresh as a daisy

as gentle as a lamb
as glorious as the sun
as good as gold
as grave as a judge

as hairy as a gorilla
as happy as a lark
as hard as nails
as heavy as lead

as illusive as a drew
as immense as the sea
as industrious as a beaver
as innocent as a lamb
as invisible as the air

as keen as mustard
as killing as a plague

as lasting as the pyramids
as lifeless as the grave
as light as air; as a feather

as loud as thunder

as mean as a miser
as meek as a dove
as merry as a lark

as natural as life
as new as day

as obstinate as a mule
as old as Methuselah
as open as a smile
as opposite as the poles

as pale as death
as patient as Job
as playful as a puppy
as poor as a church mouse
as proud as a peacock
as pure as winter snow

as quick as lightning
as quiet as a mouse

as red as a cherry
as regular as the clock
as relentless as fate
as ruthless as the sea

as shallow as a pan
as shameful as sin
as sharp as a razor
as silent as the grave
as slippery as an eel
as sly as a fox
as smooth as velvet
as steady as a rock
as sweet as honey
as swift as a deer

as tenacious as a bulldog
as thick as thieves

as thin as a rake
as timid as a rabbit
as transparent as glass

as ugly as sin
as uncertain as the weather
as unprofitable as smoke
as unreal as a dream

as vain as a peacock
as venomous as a snake
as virtuous as holy truth

as wan as moonlight
as weak as water
as wise as Solomon

cs Some of these similes have now become clichés.

Cliché: A term that has been used so many times that it has lost its significance. It is therefore highly recommended that one should avoid using those terms that are now clichés as they make one's work appear dull and unimaginative. Instead, be original and creative.

SECTION TWO
GENERAL KNOWLEDGE

FOREIGN PHRASES

Ad hoc (L.).   For this purpose, special.
Ad infinitum (L.).   To infinity.
Ad interim (L.).   In the meantime.
Ad valorem (L.).   According to the value.
Affaire d'amour (Fr.).   A love affair.
A la mode (Fr.).   According to the custom or fashion.
Al fresco (It.).   In the open air, out-of-doors.
Alter ego (L.).   Another self.
Au revoir (Fr.).   Till we meet again.
Á volonté (Fr.).   At pleasure.

Beau monde (Fr.).   The world of fashion.
Bonhomie (Fr.).   Good-nature; artlessness.
Bon vivant (Fr.).   One who lives well; a gourmand.

Causus belli (L.).   That which causes or justifies war.
Caveat emptor (L.).   Let the buyer beware (or look after his own interest).
Compos mentis (L.).   Sound of mind, sane.
Compte rendu (Fr.).   An account rendered, a report or statement drawn up.
Contretemps (Fr.).   An unlucky accident; a hitch.
Cordon bleu (Fr.).   A blue ribbon, a cook of the highest class.
Corpus delicti (L.).   The body or substance of a crime or offence.
Corrigenda (L.).   Corrections in a book.
Coup de grace (Fr.).   A finishing stroke.
Coup d'état (Fr.).   A sudden decisive blow in politics; a stroke of policy.

De facto (L.).   In fact, actual or actually.
De jure (L.).   Rightful, by right.
Deo volente (L.).   God willing.
Double entendre (Fr.).   A double meaning.
Dramatis personae (L.).   Characters in a drama or play.

En avant (Fr.).   Forward.
En déshabille (Fr.).   In undress.

Enfant terrible (Fr.).   A child who makes disconcerting remarks.

En passant (Fr.).   In passing, by the way.

En rapport (Fr.).   In harmony, in agreement; in direct relation.

Entente cordiale (Fr.).   Cordial understanding, especially between two states.

Entre nous (Fr.).   Between ourselves.

En vérité (Fr.).   In truth.

E pluribus unum (L.).   One formed out of many; out of many, one.

Esprit de corps (Fr.).   The animating spirit of a collective body, as a regiment or learned profession.

Ex cathedra (L.).   From the chair or seat of authority.

Ex officio (L.).   By virtue of his office.

Ex post facto (L.).   After the deed is done.

Fait accompli (Fr.).   A thing already done.

Faux pas (Fr.).   A false step; a mistake in behaviour.

Flagrante delicto (L.).   In the commission of the crime.

Force majeure (Fr.).   Superior power.

Hors-d'oeuvre (Fr.).   An appetizer, side dish.

In curia (L.).   In court.

In memoriam (L.).   In memory of.

Ipso facto (L.).   In the fact itself.

Labor omnia vincit (L.).   Labour conquers all.

Lapsus linguae (L.).   A slip of the tongue.

Mal a propos (Fr.).   Ill-timed; out of place.

Mardi gras (Fr.).   Shrove Tuesday.

Mea culpa (L.).   My fault.

Modus operandi (L.).   Manner of working.

Noblesse oblige (Fr.).   Rank imposes obligation; much is expected from one in good position.

Non compos mentis (L.).   Not of sound mind, insane.

Non sequitur (L.).   It does not follow.

Nota bene (L.).   Note well.

Par excellence (Fr.).   By way of eminence.

Paté de foie gras (Fr.).   Goose-liver pie.

Per se (L.).   By itself.

Poco a poco (It.).   Little by little.

Poste restante (Fr.). To be kept in the post office till called for.
Prima facie (L.). At first view or consideration.
Primus inter pares (L.). First among equals.
Pro forma (L.). As a matter of form.

Raison d'etre (Fr.). Reason for existence.
Re (L.). In the matter of.
Requiescat in pace (L.). May he (or she) rest in peace.

Sans souci (Fr.). Without care.
Savoir-faire (Fr.). Knowing how to behave.
Sine die (L.). Without a day being appointed.
Sine qua non (L.). Indispensable condition.
Sotto voce (It.). In an undertone.
Sub judice (L.). Under consideration.

Tete-a-tete (Fr.). A private conversation.
Tour de force (Fr.). A feat of strength or skill.

Verbatim (L.). Word for word.
Videlicet (viz.) (L.). Namely.
Vita brevis, ars longa (L.). Life is short, art is long.
Vox populi, vox Dei (L.). The voice of the people is the voice of God.

ABBREVIATIONS

A.A. Automobile Association
A.A.A. Amateur Athletic Association
A.A.F. Auxiliary Air Force
A and M. Ancient and Modern (Hymns)
A.B. Able-bodied seaman
abbr. abbreviation
ab init. *ab initio* (from the beginning)
abl. ablative
Abp. Archbishop
abr. abridged
a/c. account
A.C. alternating current

acc. accusative; account; according
ad. advertisement
A.D. *Anno Domini* (in the year of our Lord)
A.D.C. aide-de-camp
ad fin. *Ad finem* (towards the end)
ad inf. *ad infinitum* (to infinity)
ad init. *ad initium* (at the beginning)
ad lib. *ad libitum* (at pleasure)
ad val. *ad valorem* (according to value)
A.E.A. Atomic Energy Authority
aet. *aetatis* (of age, aged)

A.E.U. Amalgamated Engineering Union

A.F. Admiral of the Fleet

afft. affidavit (written statement)

Ag. silver

agric. agriculture

Al. aluminium

Ala. Alabama

Alas. Alaska

alg. algebra

a.l.s. autograph letter signed

a.m. *ante meridiem* (before noon)

A.M.D.G. *ad majorem Dei gloriam* (to the greater glory of God)

Amer. Ind. American Indian

amp. ampere

anc. ancient

anon. anonymous

A.N.Z.A.C. Australian and New Zealand Army Corps

A.P. Associated Press

app. appendix

appro. approval; approbation

approx. approximate, approximately

Apr. April

arch. architecture

Ariz. Arizona

Ark. Arkansas

arr. arrival; arranged

A.S. Anglo-Saxon

A.S.C. American Society of Cinematographers

A.S.L.I.B. Association of Special Libraries and Information Bureau

Assoc. Association

Asst. Assistant

Att. Gen. Attorney General

atty. attorney

Au. gold

aug. augment

Aug. August

a.u.n. *absque ulla nota* (unmarked)

A.V. Authorized Version

avdp. avoirdupois

A.W.O.L. absent without offical leave

ax. axiom; axis

b. born; book

B. black (of pencil lead)

bal. balance

Bart. Baronet

batt. battery

BB, BBB. double, treble, black (of pencil lead)

B.B.C. British Broadcasting Corporation

bbl. barrel

B.C. before Christ; British Columbia

bds. boards (in bookbinding)

b.f. bold face (type); brought forward

b.h.p. brake horse-power

b.l. bill of lading

B.M.A. British Medical Association

B.O. body odour

bot. bought; botany

B.P. British Pharmacopoeia

Bp. Bishop

brev. brevet

Brig.-Gen. Brigadier-General

Brit. Britain, British

Bros. brothers

b.s. bill of sale

b.s.g.d.g. *brevete sans garantie du gouvernement* (patented without government guarantee)

B.S.T. British Summer Time

B.Th.U. British thermal unit
B.V.M. *Beata Virgo Maria* (the Blessed Virgin Mary)

c. caught; cent; century; chapter
C. *centum* (a hundred); Centigrade
C.A.B. Civil Aeronautics Board
Cal(if). California
Can. Canada
caps. capital letter
Capt. Captain
Card. Cardinal
C.B.E. Commander of (the Order of) the British Empire
c.c. cubic centimetre
C.D. Civil Defence
c.d.v. *cartè de visite* (visiting card)
cf. *confer* (compare)
C.I.D. Criminal Investigation Department
c.i.f. cost, insurance, freight
C-in-C. Commander-in-Chief
circ. *circa, circiter* (about)
C.J. Chief Justice
cl. centilitre; class; classical
cm. centimetre
C.M.G. Companion of (the Order of) St. Michael and St. George
C.N.D. Campaign for Nuclear Disarmament
c/o. care of
C.O. commanding officer; conscientious objector
Co. Company
C.O.D. cash on delivery
C. of E. Church of England
col. column
Colo. Colorado
Conn. Connecticut
Cons. Consul
c.p. candle power

Cpl. Corporal
C.P.O. Chief Petty Officer
C.S. Civil Service
cum. cumulative
cum d., cum div. cum (with) dividend
C.V.O. Commander of the (Royal) Victorian Order
cwt. hundredweight

d. date; daughter; depart
D.C. *da capo* (repeat from the beginning); direct current; District of Columbia
D.C.M. Distinguished Conduct Medal
D.D.T. dichloro-diphenyl-trichloroethane (an insecticide)
Dec. December
deg. degree
Del. Delaware
dept. department
Deut. Deuteronomy
diam. diametre
dim. diminutive
dm. decimetre
do. *ditto* (the same)
doz. dozen
Dr. doctor; debtor
dram. pers. *dramatis personae* (characters of the play)
D.S.M. Distinguished Service Medal
D.S.O. Distinguished Service Order
D.V. *Deo volente* (God willing)
dyn. dynamics

E. East
E. & O.E. errors and omissions excepted

61

E.C.   Established Church
Eccles.   Ecclesiastes
ed.   editor, edit
Edin.   Edinburgh
E.E.C.   European Economic Community
E.F.T.A.   European Free Trade Association
e.g.   *exempli gratia* (for example)
elect.   electricity; election
E.M.F.   electromotive force
E.P.   electroplate
E.P.N.S.   electroplated nickel silver
E.P.T.   excess profits tax
esp.   especially
Esq.   Esquire
E.S.T.   Eastern Standard Time
E.T.A.   estimated time of arrival
etc.   *et cetera* (and so forth)
et seq.   *et sequens* (and what follows)
ex.   example
exc.   except
ex div.   ex dividend
exp.   export

f.   foot, feet; feminine; *forte* (loud)
F.   fine (of pencil lead); French
F., Fahr.   Fahrenheit
F.A.   Football Association
f.a.a.   free of all average
F.B.I.   Federal Bureau of Investigation
fcap, fcp.   foolscap
F.D.   *Fidei Defensor* (Defender of the Faith)
Feb.   February
fec.   *fecit or fecerunt* (made)
ff.   *fortissimo* (very loud)
f.g.a.   free of general average
fig.   figure
fin.   *ad finem* (towards the end)

Fla.   Florida
Flt-Lt, -Sgt.   Flight-Lieutenant, -Sergeant
F.M.   Field Marshall
F.O.   Foreign Office
f.o.b.   free on board
Fr.   French
fr.   franc(s)
Fri.   Friday
FTAA   Free Trade Assocoiation of America
fur.   furlong

g.   acceleration due to gravity; gram(s)
Ga.   Georgia
G.A.T.T.   General Agreement on Tariffs and Trade
G.C.   George Cross
G.C.F.   greatest common factor
Gen.   General; Genesis
G.H.Q.   General Headquarters
G.M.   George Medal
gm.   gramme(s)
G.M.T.   Greenwich mean time
G.P.   general practitioner
G.P.O.   General Post Office
gym.   gymnasium, gymnastic

h.   hour(s); height
H.   hard (of pencil lead)
h & c.   hot and cold (water)
HB.   hard black (of pencil lead)
H.C.F.   Highest Common Factor
H.E.   His/Her Excellency
hf bd.   half bound
H.H.   His/Her Highness; His Holiness
H.H.   double hard (of pencil lead)
H.J.S.   *hic jacet sepultus* (here lies, buried)
H.M.   His/Her Majesty
Hon.   Honorary; Honourable

h.p. high pressure; hire purchase; horse-power; half pay
H.Q. Headquarters
hr(s). hour(s)
H.R.H. His/Her Royal Highness
H.S.E. *hic sepultus est* (here is buried)
h.t. high tension
ht wt. hit wicket
H.W.M. high water mark

I. Idaho; Island
Ia. Iowa
I.A.T.A. International Air Transport Association
Ib., ibid. *ibidem* (in the same place)
i/c. in charge
id. *idem* (same)
i.e. *id est* (that is)
i.h.p. indicated horse-power
I.H.S. Jesus
Ill. Illinois
I.L.O. International Labour Organization
in. inch(es)
Inc. Incorporated
incog. incognito
infra dig. *infra dignitatem* (beneath one's dignity)
I.N.R.I. *Jesus Nazarenus Rex Judaeorum* (Jesus of Nazareth, King of the Jews)
inst. instant (present month)
I.O.U. I owe you
I.Q. intelligence quotient
I.R.A. Irish Republican Army
Is. Islands
I.T.A. Initial Teaching Alphabet
ital. italic (type)

J. Judge; Justice
Jam. Jamaica

Jan. January
J.P. Justice of the Peace
Jr. Junior
jun. Junior

Kan. Kansas
kc. kilocycle
kg. kilogram(s)
K.G. Knight of the Garter
K.K.K. Klu Klux Klan
kl. kilolitre
km. kilometre
Knt. Knight
K.O. knock-out
kv. kilovolt
kw. kilowatt(s)
Ky. Kentucky

L. Latin; learner (on motor vehicle); Roman numeral = 50
La. Louisiana
Lab. Labour, Labrador
lab. laboratory
Lancs. Lancashire
lat. latitude
l.b. leg-bye
lb. *libra(e)* (pound weight)
l.b.w. leg before wicket
l.c. lower case (of print)
l.h.s. left hand side
Lib. Liberal
Lieut. Lieutenant
L.J. Lord Justice
log. logarithm
long. longitude
l.p. low pressure; long primer; large paper; long-playing (record)
l.s. locus sigilli (the place of the seal)
L.S.D. lysergic acid diethylomide
l.t. low tension
Lt. Lieutenant
Ltd. Limited

L.W.M.   low-water mark

Maj.   Major
Maj.-Gen.   Major-General
Mar.   March
Mass.   Massachusetts
matric.   matriculation
M.C.   Master of Ceremonies
Md.   Maryland
Me.   Maine
memo.   memorandum
Messrs.   *Messieurs* (Gentlemen)
met.   meteorology
mf.   *mezzo forte* (half loud)
mg.   milligram(s)
Mich.   Michigan
Minn.   Minnesota
misc.   miscellaneous
Miss.   Mississippi
M.I.T.   Massachusetts Institute of Technology
mk.   mark
ml.   millilitre(s)
Mlle.   Mademoiselle, Miss
mm.   millimetre(s)
Mme.   Madame
M.O.   Medical Officer; money order
Mo.   Missouri
Mon.   Monday
Mont.   Montana
M.P.   Member of Parliament; Military Police
m.p.g.   miles per gallon
m.p.h.   miles per hour
MSS.   manuscripts
Mt.   Mount
M.V.   motor vessel

N.   North
N.A.AC.P.   National Association for the Advancement
of Coloured People
N.A.L.G.O.   National and Local Government Officers' Association
N.A.T.O.   North Atlantic Treaty Organization
naut.   nautical
N.B.   *nota bene* (note well)
N.C.   North Carolina
N.C.O.   non-commissioned officer
n.d.   no date; not dated
N.Dak.   North Dakota
N.E., NE.   North-East(ern)
Neb(r).   Nebraska
neg.   negative
nem. con.   *nemine contradicente* (no one contradicting)
Neth.   Netherlands
Nev.   Nevada
N.H.   New Hampshire
N.J.   New Jersey
N. Mex.   New Mexico
no.   *numero* (number)
nom.   nominal
non. seq.   *non-sequitur* (it does not follow)
Nov.   November
nr.   near
N.S.P.C.C.   National Society for the Prevention of Cruelty to Children
N.T.   New Testament
N.U.T.   National Union of Teachers
N.W., NW.   North-West(ern)
N.Y.(C.).   New York (City)
N.Z.   New Zealand

o/a.   on account
O.A.S.   Organization of American States
ob.   *obiit* (died)

64

obdt. obedient

O.B.E. Officer of the (Order of the) British Empire

O.C. Officer Commanding

Oct. October

O.E.C.D. Organization for Economic Cooperation and Development

O.H.M.S. On His/Her Majesty's Service

O.K. all correct

Okla. Oklahoma

o.p. out of print

op. opus

op. cit. *opere citato* (in the work quoted)

O.P.E.C. Organization of Petroleum Exporting Countries

opp. opposite

ord. order; ordinary

Ore(g). Oregon

O.S. outsize; Ordnance Survey

O.T. Old Testament

oz. ounce(s)

p. page; particle; past

p.a. per annum

Pa, Penn. Pennsylvania

P.A. Press Association; Postal Agency

P.& O. Peninsular & Oriental (Steamship Company)

par. paragraph

P.A.Y.E. pay as you earn

p.c. per cent; postcard

P.E.N. (International Association of) Poets, Playwrights, Editors, Essayists and Novelists

pen(in). peninsula

pf. *piano forte* (soft, then loud)

pl. place; plural

p.m. *post meridiem* (after noon)

P.M. Prime Minister

p.m.h. production per man-hour

P.O. Post Office; postal order; Petty Officer; Pilot Officer

pop. population

P.O.W. prisoner of war

p.p. past participle

P.P. parcel post

pp. pages

P.P.E. Politics, Philosophy and Economics (Oxford)

P.P.S. *post postscriptum* (further postscript)

pref. preference; preface

prep. preparation; preposition

Pres. President

P.R.O. Public Relations Officer

Prof. Professor

prop. proposition

pro tem. *pro tempore* (for the time)

P.S. postscript

P.T. Physical Training

Pte. Private

P.T.O. please turn over

pty. proprietary

q. query

Q.B. Queen's Bench

Q.C. Queen's Counsel

q.e.d. *quod erat demonstrandum* (which was to be demonstrated)

q.e.f. *quod erat faciendum* (which was to be done)

qr. quarter

Q.S. Quarter Session

qt. quart (s)

quot. quotation

q.v. *quod vide* (which see): *quantum vis* (as much as you wish)

R.A.D.A. Royal Academy of Dramatic Art
R.C. Roman Catholic
R.D. refer to drawer
rd. road
recd. received
ref. reference
repr. reprinted; represent
rev. revolution
Rev(d). Reverend
R.I.P. *requiescat in pace* (may he/ she rest in peace)
rom. roman (type)
r.p.m. revolutions per minute
Rt. Hon. Right Honourable
Rt. Rev. Right Reverend

S. South
Sat. Saturday
S.C. South Carolina
sch. school; scholar
s.d. several dates
S. Dak. South Dakata
sec. second
Sec. secretary
sect. section
Sen. Senator; Senate; Senior
Sept. September
Sergt. Sergeant
S.H.A.P.E. Supreme Headquarters Allied Powers in Europe
S.J. Society of Jesus (Jesuits)
S.M.O. Senior Medical Officer
Soc. Society; Socialist
S.P.C.K. Society for Promoting Christian Knowledge
sq. square
Sr. Senior
s.s. steamship
S.S.W., SSW. South-South-West
St. Street; Saint
Sun. Sunday

sup. superlative
suppl. supplement
Supt. Superintendent

T.B. tuberculosis
Tenn. Tennessee
Tex. Texas
Thurs. Thursday
T.N.T. trinitrotoluene
Treas. Treasurer
T.U.C. Trades Union Congress
Tues. Tuesday

U.F.O. unidentified flying object
U.N. United Nations
U.N.E.S.C.O. United Nations Educational, Scientific and Cultural Organization
Univ. University
U.P. United Press
U.S.S.R. Union of Soviet Socialist Republics
Ut. Utah

v. verse; versus (against)
Va. Virginia
V.D. venereal disease
Ven. Venerable
verb. sap. *verbum sapienti* (a word is enough to the wise)
V.H.F., VHF. very high frequency
V.I.P. Very Important Person
viz. *videlicet* (namely)
vol. volume
vv. verses

W. West
Wash. Washington
w.c. water closet
Wed. Wednesday
W.H.O. World Health Organization
Wisc. Wisconsin

W/L.	wave-length
W/T.	wireless telegraphy
wt.	weight
W. Va.	West Virginia
Wyo.	Wyoming
Xmas.	Christmas

Y.M.C.A. Young Men's Christian Association

yr(s). year(s); your(s)

Y.W.C.A. Young Women's Christian Association

ABBREVIATIONS (CARIBBEAN)

A.D.A.S.C. Anti-Dumping and Subsidies Commission

A.J.A. Air Jamaica Airways

B.I.T.U. Bustamante Industrial Trade Union (Jam.)

C.A.I.C. Caribbean Association of Industry and Commerce

C.A.R.I.C.O.M. Caribbean Common Market

C.A.R.I.F.E.S.T.A. Caribbean Festival of the Arts

C.A.S.E. College of Agriculture Science & Education

C.C.C. Caribbean Cement Company

C.C.H. Caciques Crown of Honour

C.C.L.T.A. Commonwealth Caribbean Lawn Tennis Association

C.C.N. Constabulary Communication Network

C.C.V. Caciques Crown of Valour

C.D. Commander of the Order of Distinction (Jam.)

C.D.B. Caribbean Development Bank

C.I.O. Congress of Undustrial Organization

C.M.U. Crime Management Unit

C.S.M.E. Caribbean Single Market Economy

C.&.W.J. Cable and Wireless Jamaica

D.L.P. Democratic Labour Party

D.S.S. Disciplined Services Star

E.D. Efficiency Decoration

E.R.D. Emergency Reserve Decoration

F.I.N.S.A.C. Financial Sector Adjustment Company

F.N.M. Freedom National Movement

G.C.T. General Consumption Tax

G.R.U.L.A.C. Group of Latin American & Caribbean Countries

H.S.M.A. Hotel Sales Managers' Association

J.A.A. Jamaica Automobile Association

J.A.L.G.O. Jamaica Association of Local Government Officers

J.A.P.A.X. Jamaica Product Exchange

J.A.S. Jamaica Agricultural Society

J.A.S.A.P. Jamaica Association of Secretaries & Administrative Professionals

J.A.V.A. Jamaica Association of Villas and Apartments

J.D.F. Jamaica Defence Force
J.F.F. Jamaica Football Federation
J.H.T.A. Jamaica Hotel and Tourist Association
J.I.S. Jamaica Information Service
J.L.A. Jamaica Livestock Association
J.L.P. Jamaica Labour Party
J.M.A. Jamaica Manufacturers' Association
J.M.M.B. Jamaica Money Market Brokers
J.P. Justice of the Peace
J.P.S. Jamaica Public Service
J.S.E. Jamaica Stock Exchange
J.T.A. Jamaica Teachers' Association
J.T.B. Jamaica Tourist Board
J.T.T.A. Jamaica Transport and Travel Association
J.U.T.C Jamaica Urban Transit Company

K.I.W. Kingston Industrial Works
K.S.A.C. Kingston and St. Andrew Corporation

L.I.A.T. Leeward Islands Air Transport
L.I.C.J. Land Information Council of Jamiaca

M.C.P. Member of Common Parliament
M.S.M. Meritorious Service Medal

N.C.U. Northern Caribbean University
N.D.M. National Democratic Movement

N.D.T.C. National Dance Theatre Company (Jam.)
N.S.T.C. Nova Scotia Technical College

O.D. Order of Distinction
O.J. Order of Jamaica
O.N. Order of the Nation (Jam.)
O.P. of the Order of Preachers, Dominicans
O.St.J. Order of St. John
O.U.R. Office of Utilities Regulation

P.L.P. Progressive Labour Party; Progressive Liberal Party
P.M. Prime Minister; Post Master
P.N.C. Peoples National Congress
P.N.M. People's National Movement
P.N.P. People's National Party
P.P.P. People's Progressive Party
P.T.T.I. Postal Telegraph and Telephone International
P.U.P. People's United Party
P.W.D. Public Works Department

R.A.D.A. Rural Agricultural Development Authority
R.J.R. Radio Jamaica (and Rediffusion)
R.S.E.S. Refrigeration Service Engineers' Society
R.T.C. Royal Technical College

S.C. Senior Council (Guyana)
S.D.C. Social Development Commission (Jam.)
S.E.B. Securities Exchange of Barbados
S.L.S. Sworn Land Surveyor
S.M.A. Sugar Manufacturers' Association

S.T.A.T.I.N. Statistical Institute

T.A.A. Trinidad Automobile Association
T.C.O. Trinidad Central Oilfields
T.C.W.S. Trinidad Central Water Scheme
T'dad. Trinidad
T.L.L. Trinidad Leasehold Ltd.
T.P.D. Trinidad Petroleum Development
T.T.S.E. Trinidad & Tobago Stock Exchange
T.V.J. Television Jamaica

U.B.O.T. United British Oilfields of Trinidad
U.B.P. United Bahamian Party
U.H.W.I. University Hospital of the West Indies
U.T.E.C.H. University of Technology
U.W.I. University of the West Indies

W.I.C.B.C. West Indies Cricket Board of Control
W.I.G.U.T. West Indies Group of University Teachers

QUOTATIONS

Adams, Henry

Adams, Henry
They know enough who know how to learn.

Aeschylus
He hears but half who hears one party only.

Alcott, Amos Bronson
Civilisation degrades the many to exalt the few.

Amiel, Henri Frédéric
A belief is not true because it is useful.

Anon
A skirt that dips behind is the outward and visible sign of inward deficiencies — as is also a collar fastened visibly with a pin.

Antoninus, Marcus Aurelius
Do not spend your thoughts upon other people, nor pry into the talk, fancies and projects of another.
Whatever anyone does or says, I must be good.

Aristotle
What we have to learn to do, we learn by doing it.
The roots of education are bitter, but the fruit is sweet.

Man is by nature a political animal.
Attitude of mind, rather than physical ability determines
      whether we succeed or fail.

Arnold, George
The living need more charity than the dead.

Arnold, George

Arnold, Matthew
The men of culture are the true apostles of equality.
Truth sits upon the lips of dying men.

Bacon, Francis
A wise man will make more opportunities than he finds.
Crafty Men condemn Studies; Simple Men admire them;
      and Wise Men use them.
Knowledge itself is power.
Reading maketh a full man; conference a ready man; and writing an exact man.

Baldwin, James
It is a great shock at the age of five or six to find that
      in a world of Gary Coopers you are the Indian.

Banda, Hastings
I wish I could bring Stonehenge to Nyasaland to show
      there was a time when Britian had a savage culture.

Baldwin, James

Barrett, Eaton Stannard
The gentleness of perfect freedom can only be won by the
      discipline of self restraint.

Beckett, Samuel
We all are born mad. Some remain so.

Bennett, Enoch Arnold
It is easier to go down a hill than up, but the view is best from the top.

Bible
Be ye therefore as wise as a serpent and harmless as doves.
A prophet is not without honour save in his own country and his own house.

Blumenthal, Oscar
Sociability is the art of unlearning to be
    preoccupied with yourself.

Buchwald, Art
Ascot is so exclusive that it's the only racecourse in the
    world where the horses own the people.

Buchwald, Art

Buddha
A man should first direct himself the way he should go.
    Only then should he instruct others.

Burdette, Robert
Don't believe the world owes you a living. It owes you nothing; it was here first.

Campbell-Bannerman, Sir Henry
This is not the end of me.

Camus, Albert
All modern revolutions have ended in a reinforcement of the power of the state.

Chesterton, G.K.
Bigotry may be roughly defined as the anger
    of men who have no opinions.

Churchill, Charles
By different methods different men excel;
    But where is he who can do all things well?

Churchill, Winston

Churchill, Winston
It is a fine thing to be honest but is also very important to be right.
Never in the field of human conflict was so much owed by
    so many to so few.

Cicero, Marcus Tullius
Natural ability without education has oftener raised man to glory
    and virtue, than education without natural ability.

Confucius
In all things, success depends upon previous preparations, and without such
    preparations there is sure to be failure.

Learning without thought is labour lost; thought without learning is perilous.
Men's natures are alike; it is their habits that carry them far apart.
Study the past, if you would divine the future.

Corneille, Pierre
He who forgives readily only invites offence.

Coward, Noel
We know what we belong to, where we come from,
and where we are going. We may not know it
with our brains but we know it with our roots.

Cowper, William

Cowper, William
A life of ease is a difficult pursuit.

Curtis, G.W.
Imagination is as good as many voyages... and much cheaper!

Diogenes
The foundation of every state is the education of its youth.

Doyle, Sir Arthur Conan
It is a capital mistake to theorize before one has data.
Different 'races' have dominated the civilized world at different historical epoch.
Don't tell people your troubles. Half of them aren't interested, and the other
half are glad you're getting what's coming to you.

Edison, Thomas Alva
Genius is one per cent inspiration and ninety-nine per cent perspiration.
Education is an ornament in prosperity and a refuge in adversity.
Education is like gold. When you want it, you have to do some digging for it is
rarely available on the surface.

Einstein, Albert
Only a life lived for others is a life worthwhile.
Eloquence is the child of knowledge.

Emerson, Ralph Waldo
Nothing astonishes men so much as common sense and
plain dealing.

Einstein, Albert

72

Epictetus
Nothing great is produced suddenly, since not
    even the grape or the fig is.

Fellini
Accept me as I am; only then will we discover each other.

France, Anatole
The Kingdom of God lies not in words but in good deeds.

Franklin, Benjamin

Franklin, Benjamin
Experience keeps a dear school, but fools will learn in no other.
Hear no ill of a friend nor speak any of an enemy.
The golden age never was the present age.
To lengthen thy life, lessen thy meals.

Freud, Sigmund
We believe that civilization has been built up, under the pressure for the struggle
    for existence, by sacrifices in gratification of the primitive impulses.

Goethe, Johann Wolfgang Von
Only within the circle of Law can there be true freedom.
Good advice is the second mother of a child.
Great minds have purposes, others have wishes.
Great opportunities come to those who make the most of the small ones.
Half education is better than complete illiteracy.

Hazlitt, William
There is a division of labour, even in vice; some persons addict themselves to the
    speculation only, others to the practice.
Rules and models destroy genius and art.
Health lies in labour and there is no royal road to it but through toil.
He who seeks the downfall of others falls first.

Hitler, Adolf
I go the way that Providence dictates with the
    assurance of a sleepwalker.

Hoch, Edward
There is so much good in the worst of us, and so much bad
in the best of us, that it hardly becomes any of us, to talk
    about the rest of us.

Hoch, Edward

73

Homer

Light is the task when many share the toil.

Hugo, Victor

Right and Law are two great forces whose harmony give birth
   to order, but their antagonism is the source of all catastrophe.
Human beings are not born equal....only when all have equal opportunity for
   achievement can it be discovered which are able and which are incompetent.
   Even then ability and incompetence are determined so largely by learning and
   habit that hereditary differences fail to explain differences in individual performance.

Hume, David

Avarice, the spur of industry.

Hume, David

Huxley, Aldous

Facts do not cease to exist because they are ignored.
Living is an art; and to practise it well, men need not only
   acquire skill, but also a native tact and taste.
Silence is full of potential wisdom and wit as unhewn marble
   of great sculpture.
That all men are equal is a proposition to which, at ordinary
times, no sane individual has ever given his assent.
The proper study of mankind is books.

Inge, William Ralph

Literature flourishes best when it is half a trade and half an art.
It is better to be a has-been than one of the never-wases.
It is costly wisdom that is bought by experience.
It's better to sleep on your plans for tomorrow than
   to stay awake over what you did today.
Inflation is when, after you finally get the money to
   buy something, it isn't enough.

Huxley, Aldous

Jami

It is easier to uproot a mountain with a needle than to
   eradicate pride from the heart of a man.

Johnson, Samuel

What is written without effort is in general read without pleasure.
Language is the dress of thought.

The law is the last result of human wisdom acting upon
    human experience for the benefit of the public.

Kaunda, Kenneth
The inability of those in power to still the voices of their own
    consciences is the great force leading to desired changes.

Kennedy, John
Those who foolishly sought power by riding on the back
    of the tiger ended up inside.

Kennedy, Robert
Some people see things and ask why. I see things and ask why not.

Kingsley, Charles
All but God is changing day by day.
Knowledge in youth is wisdom in age.

Lawrence, D.H.
Once God was all negroid, as now he is fair.
Learn from your own mistakes — but don't get
    ALL your education that way.

Letterman, Elmer
Luck is what happens when preparation meets opportunity.

Lincoln, Abraham

Lincoln, Abraham
Tact is the ability to describe others as they see themselves.
Better to remain silent and be thought a fool than to
    speak out and remove all doubt.
You can fool all the people some of the time and some of the
    people all the time, but you cannot fool all the people all the time.

Malcolm X
Only those who have already experienced a revolution
    within themselves can reach out effectively to help others.

Marx, Karl
Without doubt machinery has greatly increased the number
    of well-to-do idlers.
Men must read for amusement as well as knowledge.

Malcolm X

Maugham, Somerset
Money is like a sixth sense without which you cannot make
    a complete use of the other five.

Meredith, George
More brain, O Lord, more brain!

Meredith, George

Mills, John Stuart
As often as study is cultivated by narrow minds, they will
    draw from it narrow conclusions.
The despotism of custom is everywhere the standing hindrance
    to human advancement.
No one can make you feel inferior without your consent.

Nehru
The only alternative to co-existence is co-destruction.

Nkrumah, Kwame
Wherever there is economic dependence there is no freedom.
There is much to be done in the country with regards to industrialisation and
    development. And we need our own specialists to attend to this. See to it that
    you are on the job when the time comes.
To the men I say, assist the women to take an active part in the political life of the
    country, for remember, no country can be truly democratic in which women
    do not have equality with men.

Ovid
Ill habits gather by unseen degrees,
    as brooks make rivers, rivers run to seas.
Only the educated are free.
Old prejudices can die with those who hold them if new
    generations learn the facts.

Plato
Every king springs from a race of slaves, and every slave
    has had kings among his ancestors.
Man was not born for himself but for his country.
Our object in the construction of the state is the greatest
    happiness of the whole, and not that of any one class.
Pleasures are transient, honours are immortal.

Nkrumah, Kwame

Pliny, Gaius P. Secundus
There is always something new from Africa.

Plutarch
It is indeed desirable to be well descended, but the glory belongs to our ancestors.
Politeness is the art of choosing among one's real thoughts.

Pope, Alexander
To err is human, to forgive, divine.
True ease in writing comes from art, not chance.
Prejudice is the child of ignorance.
Know then thyself, presume not God to scan,
    The proper study of mankind is man.
Wealth and poverty are simple degrees of greed: the rich covet
    nothing, but the poor covet everything.

Pope, Alexander

Protagoras
Man is the measure of all things.

Ruskin, John
If a book is worth reading, it is worth buying.
It is only by labour that thought can be made healthy and only
    by thought can labour be made happy.

Santayana, George
Fanaticism consists in redoubling your efforts when you have forgotten your aim.
Those who cannot remember the past are condemned to repeat it.

Shakespeare, William
How poor are they that have not patience!
What wound did ever heal but by degrees?
Sweet are the uses of adversity.
Brevity is the soul of wit.

Shardun, Tijor
Faith has need of the whole truth.

Shaw, George Bernard
All great truths begin as blasphemies.
Activity is the only road to knowledge.
Liberty means responsibility. That is why most men dread it.
Simply having children does not make mothers.

Shakespeare, William

Smith, Sydney
Poverty is no disgrace to a man, but it is confoundedly inconvenient.
No furniture so charming as books.

Smollett, Tobias
Facts are stubborn things.

Smollett, Tobias

Socrates
[Four things belong to a judge:]
To hear courteously,
    to answer wisely,
    to consider soberly,
    and to decide impartially.
Solitude is the nurse of wisdom.

Sophocles
A lie never lives to be old.

Steele, Sir Richard
Reading is to the mind what exercise is to the body.

Swift, Jonathan
Books, the children of the brain.
The best doctors in the world are Doctor Diet,
    Doctor Quiet and Doctor Merryman.

Swift, Jonathan

Syrus, Publilius
It matters not what you are thought to be, but what you are.

Taylor, Jane
Though man a thinking being is defined, few use
    the grand prerogative of the mind.

Tennyson, Alfred
Knowledge comes, but wisdom lingers.
The ability to stick to one thing until the job is done is a quality demonstrated more
    by postage stamps than by people.
The first quality of a good education is good manners — and some people flunk
    the course.
The ultimate in shapely curves is found in a smile.
Things have got to be wrong in order that they may be deplored.

Time is always too much for the idle.
To fool the world, tell the truth.
Toil is the sire of fame.

Twain, Mark
Soap and education are not as sudden as a massacre,
    but they are more deadly in the long run.

Twain, Mark

Voltaire
Who serves his country well has no need of ancestors.

Walker, William
Learn to read slow; all other graces will follow in their proper places.

Wallace, William Ross
The hand that rocks the cradle is the hand that rules the world.

Washington, George
Associate yourself with men of good quality if you esteem your own reputation;
    for 'tis better to be alone than in bad company.
Be courteous to all, but intimate with few, and let those few be well tried before
    you give them your confidence. True friendship is a plant of slow growth, and
    must undergo and withstand the shocks of adversity before it is entitled to the
    appellation.
Labour to keep alive in your breast that little spark of
    celestial fire, called conscience.

Webster, Daniel
When tillage begins, other arts follow. The farmers,
    therefore, are the founders of human civilization.
There is nothing so powerful as truth — and often nothing
    so strange.

Wilde, Oscar
The old believe everything; the middle-aged suspect
    everything; the young know everything.
Education is an admirable thing, but it is well to
    remember from time to time that nothing that
    is worth knowing can be taught.
Experience is the name everyone gives to his mistakes.
I have nothing to declare but my genius.

Washington, George

Williams, Dr. Eric
A small country like ours [Trinidad and Tobago]
only has principles.

Williams, Dr. Eric

Wilson, Thomas Woodrow
The history of liberty is a history of resistance.
Character is a by-product; it is produced in the great
manufacture of daily duty.
Wit does not take the place of knowledge.
Wit is the salt of conversation, not the food.

Young, Edward
Wishing, of all employments, is the worst.

FAMOUS PEOPLE

Abraham. (*c.* 2000 B.C.) First Hebrew patriarch who founded
the line that was to produce the 12 tribes of Israel.

Adams, John. (1735–1826) Second president of the United States (1797–1801). He was one of the signers of the Declaration of Independence.

Adams, John Quincy. (1767–1848) Sixth president of the
United States (1825–29). He drafted the Monroe
Doctrine and was a leading campaigner for the abolition
of slavery.

Adenauer, Konrad. (1876–1967) Chancellor of German
Federal Republic (West Germany) (1949–63). He was a
consistent anti-Nazi, and was removed from office by
Hitler.

Adler, Alfred

Adler, Alfred. (1870–1937) Austrian psychiatrist and
psychologist, originator of the concept of inferiority complex.

Adrian (Hadrian) IV. (*c.* 1100–59). The only English pope (1154–59).

Aesop. (6th cent. B.C.) Greek author of the oldest and most
famous collection of animal fables.

Alcock, Sir John. (1892–1919). English aviator who completed
the first non-stop transatlantic flight in 1919.

Alexander III (the Great). (356–323 B.C.) King of Macedon (336–323 B.C.)
whose conquests in less than ten years built an empire as big as the United
States, quadrupled the size of the world known to the Greeks, and culturally
cross fertilized Europe and Asia.

Alfred the Great. (849–899) Saxon king who halted the Danish conquest of England.

Ali, Muhammad. (1942–) American world heavyweight champion boxer who refused U.S. army draft, won his right to refuse in the courts and went on to become the world's leading boxer.

Amundsen, Roald. (1872–1928). Norwegian polar explorer, the first man to reach the South Pole and to navigate the North-West Passage.

Anastasia, Albert. (*c*.1902–57) American gangster, founder of 'Murder Inc.'

Andersen, Hans Christian. (1805–75) Danish writer, celebrated for his *Fairy Tales*.

Angelou, Maya. (1928–) Best selling Afro-American poet whose poetry is famous worldwide.

Ali, Muhammad

Antonius, Marcus. (*c*. 82–30 B.C.) Roman leader whose defeat by Octavius established rule by emperors.

Apollonius. (3rd cent. B.C.) Greek mathematician. His works formed the basis for further studies of conic sections (ellipse, parabola and hyperbola).

Aquinas, Thomas. (1225–74) Catholic philosopher and theologian. He adapted Aristotle's philosophy to Christian dogma.

Arafat, Yasser. (1929–) Born Mohammed Abdel-Raouf Arafal As Qudwa al-Hussaeini in Cairo to Palestinian parents. He became the chairman of the Palestinian Liberation (PLO) Committee in 1969.

Archimedes. (*c*. 287–212 B.C.) Greek mathematician and inventor — an important scientist of antiquity. The Archimedes principle evolved from his discovery that submerged bodies displace their own volume of liquid and have their weight diminished by the weight of liquid displaced.

Aristotle. (*c*. 384–322 B.C.) Greek philosopher. He was the inventor of logic (he called it analytics).

Armstrong, Louis. (1900–71) American Negro trumpeter. His influence on jazz was perhaps greater than any other musician.

Armstrong, Neil. (1930–) American astronaut. First man to walk on the moon at 10.56 p.m. on 20th July 1969.

Asoka. (3rd cent. B.C.) Indian king of the Maurya dynasty, whose empire covered two-thirds of the Indian subcontinent.

Atahualpa. (1500–33) Last Inca king of Peru. He was murdered by Pizzaro, the Spanish conquistador.

Armstrong, Louis

Attila. (*c*. 406–453) King of the Huns (443–453). Called the 'Scourge of God', he overran Europe from the North Sea to the Caspian.

Attlee, Clement Richard. (1883–1967) British Prime Minister (1945–51). He implemented the Welfare State and granted independence to India (1947).

Austen, Jane. (1775–1817) English novelist who wrote on the lifestyle of English country society *(Pride and Prejudice).*

Bach, Johann Sebastian.

Bach, Johann Sebastian. (1685–1750) German composer *(Mass in B Minor)* who brought European music to one of its highest peaks of achievement.

Bacon, Francis. (1561–1626) English philosopher, lawyer and author who was the first important writer of Essays in English.

Baden Powell, Robert. (1857–1941) English founder of the Boy Scout movement.

Balanchine, George. (1904–83) Russian-born choreographer, pioneer of American 'Classic' ballet.

Balboa, Vasco Núñez de. (1475–1519) Spanish explorer, the first European to see the Pacific. Settler of Haiti and Dominican Republic.

Bannister, Roger. (1929–) English athlete, the first person to run a mile in under 4 minutes.

Barnard, Christian. (1922–2001) South African surgeon, the first man to transplant a human heart (1967).

Beethoven, Ludwig van. (1770–1827) German composer who brought the symphony to its peak as a musical form.

Bell, Alexander Graham. (1847–1922) Scottish-born American who invented the telephone.

Berlin, Irving. (1888–1989) American, self-taught composer of some of the most popular songs *(White Christmas)* ever written.

Bernadette of Lourdes. (1844–79) French saint whose visions of Virgin Mary resulted in Lourdes being established as a healing shrine, a place of pilgrimage.

Bin Laden, Osama. (1957–) International terrorist linked to the bombing of US embassies in Africa in 1993, the USS Cole in Yemen and the World Trade Centre in 1993. Also, and most wanted for the September 11, 2001 terrorist attack on the World Trade Centre which saw passenger planes being flown into the twin towers.

Bin Laden, Osama

Birdseye, Clarence. (1886–1956) American industrialist who developed a technique for deep freezing foods.

Blackwell, Elizabeth. (1821–1910) American physician, first woman to qualify as a doctor of medicine.

Boccaccio, Giovanni. (1313–75) Italian writer and poet whose *Il Decameron* is one of the world's masterpieces.

Bolívar, Simón. (1783–1830) Venezuelan revolutionary leader who liberated much of South America from Spanish rule.

Boone, Daniel. (1734–1820) American frontiersman and folk hero who largely contributed to the colonization of Kentucky.

Booth, William

Booth, William. (1829–1912) British religious leader, founder of the Salvation Army.

Bradman, Sir Donald. (1908–2001) Australian cricketer and the most prolific scorer in the game. His score of 452 not out (1929–30) was a record for 29 years.

Braille, Louis. (1809–52) French inventor of the Braille system of reading for the blind. He himself was blinded at the age of 3 years.

Brown, John. (1800–59) American anti-slavery crusader; commemorated in the marching song *John Brown's Body.*

Brutus, Marcus Junius. (*c.* 85–42 B.C.) Roman, leader of the republican conspirators against Julius Caesar.

Bustamante, Sir William Alexander. (1884–1977) Jamaican politician, who withdrew his country from the West Indies Federation in 1962. He founded the Jamaica Labour Party and was Jamaica's first Prime Minister.

Bustamante, Sir William Alexander

Cabot, John. (1450–98) Venetian immigrant to England, the first of England's ocean explorers.

Cabral, Pedro Alvares. (*c.* 1460 –*c.* 1526) Portuguese navigator who discovered Brazil.

Caesar, Gaius Julius. (100–44 B.C.) Roman general and dictator of the Roman Empire.

Calvin, John. (1509–64) French theologian, founder of the Calvinist branch of the Protestant church.

Capone, Alphonso ('Al'). (1895–1947) Italian-born American gangster who built up a criminal organization during the prohibition era (1919–33). He was responsible for over 500 murders.

Carroll, Lewis. (1832–98) English mathematician and writer whose imaginative fantasies are among the most original works of their kind (*Alice in Wonderland*).

Casanova, Giovanni Jacopo. (1725–98) Italian adventurer whose exploits dazzled European high society. His bawdy memoirs are world famous.

Cassidy, Butch. (1866–1910) American cowboy and rustler who became the leader of a group of outlaws. In 1902, he sailed for South America and was later killed in Bolivia.

Castro, Fidel

Castro, Fidel. (1926–) Charismatic dictator of Cuba who has been in power for over three decades.

Cayley, Sir George. (1773–1857) English engineer and inventor, founder of the science of aerodynamics. He built the glider which made the first heavier-than-air flight.

Celsius, Anders. (1701–44) Swedish astronomer, inventor of the Centigrade temperature scale.

Chaka. (1773–1828) Zulu chieftain, founder of the Zulu empire.

Chandragupta I. (4th cent.) Indian Rajah of Magadha who founded the Gupta dynasty (320–480), the golden age of Hindu literature and art.

Chaplin, Charles. (1889–1977) English director-writer, probably the best known actor in the history of cinema.

Charlemagne. (742–814) Western (Holy Roman) Emperor who built the biggest empire in western Europe since that of Rome.

Chaucer, Geoffrey. (*c.* 1340–1400) English poet, father of English poetry. He wrote *The Canterbury Tales*.

Chekhov, Anton. (1860–1904) Russian dramatist, master of the tragi-comedy which foreshadowed trends in modern drama.

Churchill, Sir Winston Leonard Spencer. (1874–1965) British statesman, Prime Minister during the 'Battle of Britain'. He was a soldier, historian, painter and among the greatest of war leaders.

Crockett, Davy. (1786–1836) American frontiersman; member of the U.S. House of Representatives (1827–31 and 1833–35). He was killed at the Alamo.

Dickens, Charles. (1812–70) English novelist who wrote outstanding social novels of the 19th century (*Pickwick Papers, Nicholas Nickleby, Hard Times*).

Diesel, Rudolf. (1858–1913) German engineer and inventor of the internal combustion engine which bears his name.

Chaplin, Charles

Diogenes of Apollonia. (5th cent. B.C.) Greek philosopher who held that air was the basis of all things.

Disney, Walt. (1901–66) American producer of cartoon films.

Dostoevsky, Fyodor Mikhailovich. (1821–81) Russian writer of religious and philosophical themes (*The Brothers Karamazov, Crime and Punishment*).

Drake, Francis. (*c.* 1540–96) English explorer, adventurer and naval captain who circumnavigated the world. He served England by plundering Spanish treasure ships.

Disney, Walt

Dumas, Alexandre. (1802–70) French dramatist, novelist, best known for his swashbuckling historical romances (*The Three Musketeers*).

Duvalier, Francois. (1907–71) Dictator of Haiti, known as 'Papa Doc'. He was regarded by his people as the incarnation of the voodoo god, Baron Samedi.

Earp, Wyatt. (1848–1929) American 'Marshall', famous for law enforcement by gun. His crude methods helped to tame America's Wild West.

Eastman, George. (1854–1932) American inventor of the flexible roll film system of photography. He produced the Kodak camera.

Eckert, John Presper. (1919–95) American electrical engineer who, with William Mauchly, made the first electronic computer ENIAC in 1946.

Eddy, Mary Baker. (1821–1910) American religious leader and founder of the Christian Science Movement.

Ehrlich, Paul. (1854–1915) German bacteriologist who founded chemotherapy, the science of the chemical treatment of disease.

Einstein, Albert. (1879–1955) German-American physicist, who proposed the theory of relativity; this general theory led to a new era of research and his stated equation $E=MC^2$ led to the atomic bomb.

Einthoven, Willem. (1860–1927) Dutch physiologist who developed electrocardiography.

Earp, Wyatt

Elijah. (9th cent. B.C.) Hebrew prophet of Yahweh (Jehovah) who ranks with Moses as a founder of Judaism.

Empedocles. (5th cent. B.C.) Greek philosopher and physician who originated the theory of four elements — fire, air, water, earth — as the basic substance from which all else is made.

Engels, Friedrich. (1820–95) German political writer who worked with Karl Marx to formulate the theory of dialectical materialism (*Communist Manifesto,* 1848).

Epicurus. (*c.* 342–270 B.C.) Greek philosopher whose name is synonymous with luxury and an excessive love of pleasure.

Euclid. (3rd–2nd cent. B.C.) Greek mathematician who wrote *Elements*, a fundamental geometric treatise.

Ford, Henry

Fahrenheit, Gabriel. (1686–1736) German-Dutch physicist who was the first to use mercury in a thermometer, and so devised the scale for measuring temperature which bears his name.

Faraday, Michael. (1791–1867) English chemist and physicist whose discovery of electro-magnetic induction revealed the principle of the electric motor and dynamo, the transformer and the telephone.

Fawkes, Guy. (1570–1606) English Roman Catholic conspirator in the Gunpowder Plot to blow up the Houses of Parliament (1605) as a protest against the treatment of Catholics.

Fermi, Enrico. (1901–54) Italian-American physicist who built the first nuclear reactor. Its success began the age of nuclear power.

Fleming, Sir Alexander. (1881–1955) Scottish bacteriologist who, in 1928, discovered the antibiotic penicillin.

Ford, Henry. (1863–1947) American industrialist and automobile manufacturer who developed mass production assembly-line techniques to provide cheap and reliable motoring for millions of people and pioneered high-wage, high-output labour utilization.

Fournier, Pierre. (1712–68) French engraver who was the first to devise the points system for measuring and naming sizes of type.

Fox, George. (1624–91) English religious reformer, who founded the Society of Friends, commonly called the Quakers.

Freud, Sigmund. (1856–1939) Austrian psychiatrist and founder of psychoanalysis. His was the belief that forgotten or deliberately buried memories underlie all abnormal mental states.

Gagarin, Yuri. (1934–68) Russian cosmonaut who became the first man to travel in space on 12 April 1961, in *Vostok 1*. He orbited the earth in 108 minutes at a maximum velocity of 27,840 km. p.h. (17,400 m.p.h.) at an average altitude of 253 kilometres (158 miles).

Fox, George

Galilei, Galileo. (1564–1642) Italian astronomer, physicist and mathematician who discovered the principles of motion. He was the first man to perceive that mathematics and physics were parts of one area of knowledge.

Gama, Vasco da. (*c.* 1469–1525) Portuguese navigator, commander of the first fleet to sail from Europe to Asia.

Gandhi, Mohandas. (1869–1948) Principal creator of India's independence and most notable exponent of 'passive resistance'.

Garvey, Marcus Aurelius. (1887–1940) Jamaican Negro leader who was active in the United States (1916–23). Garvey was the founder of the Universal Negro Improvement Association (UNIA). He advocated racial separation and emigration of American Negroes to Africa. He was deported from the USA in 1923. In 1964 he was declared a national hero in his country.

Garvey, Marcus

Gatling, Richard. (1818–1903) American inventor of a rapid-fire machine gun, used in the later stages of the American Civil War.

Gautama, Buddha. (*c.* 563– *c.*483 B.C.) Indian-born founder of Buddhism, which claims that existence means suffering; suffering follows from desire; suffering ends when desire is extinguished.

Geiger, Hans. (1882–1945) German physicist, inventor of the Geiger counter for detecting atomic particles.

Genghis, Khan. (1162–1227) Mongol chief, one of the great conquerors in world history.

Geronimo. (1829–1909) Apache chief who led one of the last serious Indian revolts against white supremacy in North America.

Gershwin, George. (1898–1937) American composer who extended jazz into a concert idiom with his opera *Porgy and Bess.*

Goddard, Robert. (1882–1945) American physicist and pioneer of rocketry. He pioneered the use of liquified gases as rocket propellants.

Grace, William Gilbert. (1848–1915) English cricketer who was the foremost influence on modern batting and bowling techniques.

Grimm, Jacob. (1785–1863) **Grimm, Wilhelm.** (1786– 1859) German writers, widely known for their collection known a Grimm's Fairy Tales.

Goddard, Robert

Gutenberg, Johannes. (1398–1468) German goldsmith credited with the invention of printing from movable type.

Hahn, Otto. (1879–1968) German chemist who discovered nuclear fission.

Haile Selassie. (1892–1975) Emperor of Ethiopia, Lion of Judah, who succeeded Empress Zauditu in 1930. He was hailed as God by the Rastafarian sect in Jamaica.

Halley, Edmond. (1656–1742) English astronomer after whom Halley's Comet is named.

Hammurabi. (18th cent. B.C.) Babylonian king. He provided Babylonia with a written code of laws which is regarded as the first major legislative work of the forerunners of Western civilization.

Harris, Benjamin. (1673–1716) English journalist and publisher of the first newspaper printed in America.

Haile Selassie

Harvey, William. (1578–1657) English physician who discovered the process by which blood circulates in the body.

Hasan, Ali Shah. (1800–81) Persian religious leader and first holder of the hereditary title Aga Khan, spiritual head of the Nizari Ismaili sect.

Hefner, Hugh. (1926–) American businessman who founded Playboy magazine which is distributed worldwide.

Helmont, Jean Baptiste van. (1577–1644) Flemish chemist who originated the term 'gas'. He realised that there were other air-like substances in addition to air.

Hertz, Heinrich Rudolph. (1857–94) German physicist who discovered radio waves and showed that, like light waves, they can be focused and reflected.

Hiawatha. (16th cent.) Red Indian chief, founder of the Indian league.

Hillary, Sir Edmund. (1919–) New Zealand mountaineer. With Tenzing Norgay, he was the first to climb Mount Everest, in May 1953.

Hippocrates. (*c*. 460–377 B.C.) Greek physician, called the 'Father of Medicine'. His extensive descriptions formed the basis of classical medicine. The 'Hippocratic Oath' is the essential of medical ethics.

Hitler, Adolf. (1889–1945) Austrian-born Führer of the German Third Reich, whose policies plunged Europe into the Second World War.

Homer. (9th cent. B.C.) Greek legendary author of the *Iliad* and the *Odyssey.*

Houdini, Harry. (1874–1926) American magician who could escape from any bond or container.

Hillary,
Sir Edmund

Hughes, Langston. (1902–67) American author who was one of the first Negroes to win a literary reputation (*Weary Blues,* 1926).

Hunter, John. (1728–93) British physiologist and surgeon who founded scientific surgery.

Huskisson, William. (1770–1830) British Tory reformer and pioneer of free trade, and one of history's first victims of a railway accident.

Hughes, Langston

Hyatt, John Wesley. (1837–1920) American inventor who produced celluloid, the first synthetic plastic.

Ibn, Saud. (1880–1953) Creator of the kingdom of Saudi Arabia, which he subsequently took into the United Nations.

Ictinus. (5th cent. B.C.) Greek architect who is immortalised by the Parthenon which he designed with Callicrates.

Ignatius of Loyola, St. (1491–1556) Spanish founder of the Society of Jesus, or Jesuit order.

Ipatieff, Vladimir. (*c.* 1867–1952) Russian-American chemist, whose studies of high-pressure catalytic reactions were basic to the petro-chemical industry.

Jabir, ibn-Haijan. (*c.* 721–815) Arab alchemist credited with the first preparation of the poison arsenic.

James, William. (1842–1910) American philosopher who put forward the theory of pragmatism: "the truth of a concept is its successful use in practice".

Jenner, Edward. (1749–1823) English physician who developed vaccination against smallpox.

Jesus Christ. (Born between 8 B.C. and 4 B.C.; died *c.* A.D. 29) Son of God and founder of the Chrisitan faith. His preaching of love gave the world a faith that now has over 2 billion adherents.

Joan of Arc. (1412–31) French peasant girl who led an army to free Orléans. She claimed that heavenly voices gave her directives from God.

Johnson, Amy. (1903–41) English aviator, the first woman to fly solo from England to Australia.

Jordan, Michael. (1963–) Afro-American basketball star who is arguably the best to have ever played the sport of basketball.

Jordan, Michael

Kamerlingh Onnes, Heike. (1853–1926) Dutch physicist, the first person to liquefy helium. He found that at very low temperatures certain metals, such as lead and mercury, lose their electrical resistance and become super-conductors.

Kano, Jigoro. (1860–1938) Japanese founder of judo. He studied the many clan techniques of ju-jitsu and combined them to create judo.

Kennedy, John F. (1917–1963) One of the most famous U.S. presidents. He was in power at the time of the Cuban missile crisis. On November 22, 1963 Kennedy was killed by an assasin's bullet in Dallas, Texas.

Kennedy, John F

Keynes, Lord John. (1883–1946) British economist. He stressed the control of economic mechanisms to achieve desirable objectives. He was one of the chief architects of the International Monetary Fund.

Khorana, Har Gobind (1922–   ) Indian-American biochemist who manufactured the first synthetic gene.

King, Martin Luther. (1929–68) Amerian civil rights leader, whose non-violent demonstrations and passive resistance advanced the cause of the American Negroes.

Lady Diana. (1961–1997) Deceased Princess of Wales, the most photographed woman in the world. She was most recognized for her philanthropic spirit and was a pioneer in many causes including HIV/AIDS.

King, Martin Luther

Land, Edwin Herbert. (1909–91) American inventor who produced the material known as 'polaroid' which has been used in spectacles. In 1947, he invented the Polaroid camera.

Le Corbusier. (1887–1965) Swiss architect who was one of the pioneers of modern architecture.

Lee, Robert E. (1807–70) American general, commander-in-chief of the Confederate armies in the American Civil War.

Lee, William. (16th–17th cent.) English clergyman, who in 1589, invented the knitting machine.

Leonardo da Vinci. (1452–1519) The greatest figure of the Italian Renaissance — a scientist, painter (*Mona Lisa, Last Supper*).

Lincoln, Abraham. (1809–65) American president who led the American North to victory over the South in the Civil War (1861–65).

Lindbergh, Charles. (1902–74) American aviator, the first man to fly the Atlantic solo (May 1927).

Lockyer, Sir Joseph.   (1836–1920) British astronomer who discovered the element helium.

Luther, Martin.   (1483–1546) German religious reformer who challenged the Roman Church Doctrine, which helped to change the face of Christianity.

Luthuli, Albert John.   (1898–1967) South African nationalist leader who opposed racism in his country by non-violent methods. He won the Nobel Peace Prize in 1960.

Magellan, Ferdinand.   (*c.* 1480–1521) Portuguese explorer who led, for Spain, the first expedition to circumnavigate the earth. He was killed before the voyage was completed.

Mahavira. (*c.* 6th cent. B.C.) Indian founder of Jainism, an offshoot of Hinduism. The religion has a very high ethical code.

Malcolm X. (1925–1965) American civil rights leader who took a more militant approach than Marcus Aurelius Garvey to advance the cause of the American Negro.

Manby, George William.   (1765–1854) Englishman who, in 1813, invented the portable fire extinguisher.

Mandela, Nelson. (1918–) Black South African civil rights leader, who led the fight against apartheid. Went from political prisoner to president of South Africa.

Mandela, Nelson

Mao Tse-tung.   (1893–1976) Chairman of the Chinese Communist Party. After years of fighting, he drove the Nationalist forces from mainland China in 1949.

Marey, Etienne Jules.   (1830–1904) French physiologist, inventor of the cine camera, which resulted in the era of cinematography.

Marley, Bob.   (1945–1981) Internationally known Jamaican Reggae icon.

Marshall, Thurgood.   (1908–1993) American Negro judge. He was chief counsel to the National Association for the Advancement of Coloured People (1938–61). His arguments led to the ruling of 1954 — that segregation in public schools was unconstitutional.

Mao Tse-tung

Martí, José.   (1853–95) Cuban national hero, revolutionary and poet, who led the struggle for independence from Spain and was killed in the uprising.

Marx, Karl.   (1818–83) German philosopher and theorist of socialism. In collaboration with Friedrich Engels he wrote *Communist Manifesto* (1848) and *Das Kapital* (1867). The official doctrine of the Soviet Union was based on his ideas.

Matthew, St. (1st cent. A.D.) Christian apostle, born in Palestine. He was the author of the First Gospel of the New Testament.

Maxim, Sir Hiram. (1840–1916) American-born engineer. While in England he invented the fully automatic machine gun (1883).

McAdam, John Loudon. (1756–1836) Scottish engineer, leading road builder of the 19th century. His method of road building carries his name.

Mège-Mouries, Hippolyte. (1817–1880) French chemist and inventor who developed the economic method of producing margarine (a butter substitute).

Montessori, Maria

Michelangelo Buonarroti. (1475–1564) Italian painter, architect, sculptor and poet. He was the most famous figure of the Renaissance. His most famous work is on the ceilings of the Sistine Chapel in the Vatican (1508–12).

Mohammed. (570–632) Arab prophet and founder of Islam, the world religion which now has over 1.2 billion adherents.

Montessori, Maria. (1870–1952) Italian educator who advocated "free discipline" in teaching children. She taught backward children to read and write — *The Montessori Method* (1912).

Montezuma II. (*c.* 1480–1520) Aztec emperor (1502–20) of Mexico at the time of the Spanish conquest.

Morgan, Sir Henry. (*c.* 1635–88) Welsh buccaneer who became Lieutenant-Governor of Jamaica in 1674, and was given the task of ending buccaneering.

Moses. (13th cent B.C.) Hebrew prophet and lawgiver who led the Israelites from Egypt towards the Holy Land.

Myron. (5th cent. B.C.) Greek sculptor, whose *Discus Thrower* is one of the most famous sculptures of all time.

Morgan, Sir Henry

Nebuchadnezzar II. (6th cent. B.C.) Babylonian king who restored the ancient cities of Babylonia, including Babylon and its famous 'Hanging Gardens'. He drove the Egyptians out of Asia.

Nehru, Jawaharlal. (1889–1964) Indian statesman; first Prime Minister of India following her independence.

Nelson, Horatio. (1758–1805) British admiral, whose victory at the Battle of Trafalgar (1805) during the Napoleonic wars destroyed Franco-Spanish naval power.

Nero. (A.D. 37–68) Roman emperor, who massacred Rome's Christians in retribution for a fire which destroyed most of the city in A.D. 64.

Newton, Sir Isaac. (1642–1727) English mathematician and scientist who authored the laws of motion and gravity. In 1687, he published his masterpiece *Philosophiae Naturalis Principia Mathematica.*

Nkrumah, Kwame. (1909–1972) Ghanaian nationalist politician, the first President of the Republic of Ghana. He was deposed in 1966, and died in exile.

Nostradamus. (1503–66) French astrologer, physician and prophet who, it is alleged, treated the plague successfully, and became occult consultant of Catherine de Medici.

Owens, Jesse

Omar, Khayyam. (*c.*1050– *c.* 1123) Persian astronomer and poet. He wrote *The Rubáiyát* and some Arabic mathematical treatises.

Owens, Jesse. (1913–1980) American athlete who, by winning three gold medals in the 1936 Olympic Games at Berlin, disproved Hitler's theory of Aryan supremacy.

Paracelsus. (*c.* 1493–1541) Swiss physician and alchemist, who pioneered the use of arsenic, lead, mercury and iron in the chemical treatment of diseases.

Parkinson, James. (1755–1824) English physician noted for his work on the disease which bears his name (Parkinson's disease).

Pasteur, Louis. (1822–95) French chemist, whose research led to the development of modern vaccine therapy. He himself developed a vaccine against rabies.

Paterson, William. (1658–1719) British financier who founded the Bank of England.

Pavlov, Ivan. (1849–1936) Russian physiologist who is noted for his study of conditioned reflexes.

Pelé (Edison Arantes do Nascimento). (1940–) Brazilian footballer who became the first player to score 1,000 goals. He is thought of as the greatest soccer player of all times.

Perceval, Spencer. (1762–1812) The only British Prime Minister to have been assassinated.

Peter, St. (1st cent.) Leader of Jesus's disciples. His devotion to Jesus has inspired Christians in all ages.

Perceval, Spencer

Peter I 'The Great'. (1672–1725) Tsar of Russia (1682–1725). He made Russia a part of Europe and led it from being a backward country to a modern state.

Picasso, Pablo. (1881–1973) Spanish-born artist, perhaps the greatest and most widely known of modern painters.

Pitman, Sir Isaac. (1813–97) English publisher, known for his invention of the shorthand system of writing.

Pius IX. (1792–1878) The longest reigning pope (1846–78) who promulgated the dogma of papal infallibility (1870).

Pizarro, Francisco. (*c.* 1470–1541) Spanish conqueror of the Inca empire. He founded Lima after obtaining permission to conquer and govern Peru.

Plato. (*c.* 427–347 B.C.) Greek philosopher. He wrote *Republic*, a discussion on the nature of justice, the citizen and the state.

Powell, Collin

Pocahontas. (*c.* 1595–1617) American Indian princess, who saved the life of John Smith. She was converted to Christianity and married John Rolfe, an Englishman.

Polo, Marco. (*c.* 1254–*c.* 1324) Venetian who travelled extensively throughout Asia. His accounts of these travels acquainted Europeans, for the first time, with Oriental marvels, and gave an idea of China's size and wealth.

Ponce de León. (1460–1521) Spanish explorer credited with the discovery of Florida.

Powell, Collin. (1937–) Afro-American who is one of the most powerful men in the United States. He was formally Chairman of the Joint Chiefs of Staff and is currently Secretary of State in the U.S. Government.

Presley, Elvis. American pop music legend. Probably the most known singer in American pop music culture.

Pythagoras. (*c.* 582–500 B.C.) Greek philosopher. To him, "all things are numbers" and his theory became a way of life for his followers.

Queensberry, John. (1844–1900) British patron of boxing, who gave his name to the rules under which boxing matches are conducted.

Presley, Elvis

Raikes, Robert. (1735–1811) British publisher, who founded Sunday Schools (teaching of reading and catechism).

Rasputin, Grigori. (*c.* 1871–1916) Russian monk and mystic, who had great influence over Russian politics (*c.* 1911–16).

Reuter, Paul Julius von. (1816–99) German founder of one of the world's biggest news agencies.

Revere, Paul. (1735–1818) American patriot immortalised in Longfellow's poem. He rode from Boston to Lexington to warn the American militia of the British advance.

Rodney, George Brydges. (1719–92) English admiral who, as commander-in-chief of the Leeward Islands, subdued the French islands in the West Indies. He won many battles, most notably the Battle of the Saints (1782) which ended the French threat to the West Indies.

Röntgen, Wilhelm Conrad. (1845–1923) German physicist who discovered X-rays (1895).

Roosevelt, Franklin Delano. (1882–1945) American president who served an unprecedented three terms, and died in his fourth term of office. He introduced the 'New Deal' programme which legislated to liberalize and control relations between capital and labour.

Roosevelt, Franklin

Ross, Sir James Clark. (1800–62) Scottish polar explorer who discovered and located the North Magnetic Pole (1831).

Ruth, Babe. (1895–1948) American baseball hero renowned for his home run scoring (714).

Sade, Marquis de. (1740–1814) French writer renowned for his tales of sexual perversion and cruelty. The term 'sadism' is derived from him.

Saklatvala, Shapurji. (1874–1936) The first Indian and first communist to become a British Member of Parliament.

Saladin. (1138–93) Sultan of Egypt and Syria who briefly put an end to Christian crusaders' dominance in Palestine.

Ruth, Babe

Salk, Jonas Edward. (1914–1995) American microbiologist, who developed the vaccine against poliomyelitis.

San Martín, José de. (1778–1850) Argentinian revolutionary who liberated Chile and Peru from the Spaniards.

Shakur, Tupac. (1971–1996) Top selling hip hop artiste, poet and talented actor.

Tenzing, Norgay. (1914–86) Nepalese mountaineer, who with Edmund Hillary, became the first man to climb Mt. Everest, the world's highest mountain.

Terman, Lewis. (1877–1956) American psychologist who introduced the first intelligence test to be put to general use. He coined the term intelligence quotient (I.Q.).

Thomson, Sir Joseph John. (1856–1940) English physicist who discovered the electron (the first sub-atomic particle).

Torricelli, Evangelista. (1608–47) Italian physicist and mathematician who invented the barometer.

Trotsky, Leon. (1879–1940) Russian Jewish revolutionary. He created and trained the Red Army from a disorganized volunteer force, which he inspired to victory in the civil war.

Truman, Harry S. (1884–1972) Thirty-third president of the United States. He authorised the use of the atomic bomb against Japan in 1945, ending the Second World War.

Valentino, Rudolph. (1895–1926) Italian-American romantic screen actor who achieved great success after making *The Four Horsemen of the Apocalypse* and *The Sheik.*

Versace, Gianni. (1946–1997) Italian fashion designer whose bold and colourful designs are famous worldwide.

Verwoerd, Hendrik Freusch. (1910–66) Founder of the South African Republic (1961) and exponent of apartheid.

Truman, Harry S

Vincent de Paul, St. (*c.* 1581–1660) French founder of the Congregation of the Priests of the Mission and Sisters of Charity.

Volta, Count Alessandro. (1745–1827) Italian physicist who invented the electric battery.

Walsh, Courtney. (1962–) Jamaican test cricketer, who became the first player to take over 500 wickets.

Walter, John. (1739–1812) English publisher and founder of *The Times,* Britain's leading and influential newspaper.

Washington, George. (1732–99) First president of the United States. He was the leader of the American colonists in the War of Independence against Britian.

Watt, James. (1736–1819) Scottish engineer, who improved the efficiency and versatility of the steam engine which powered the Industrial Revolution.

Webb, Matthew. (1848–83) English swimmer, the first man to swim the English Channel (1875).

Weber, Max. (1864–1920) German sociologist and political economist who challenged Karl Marx's theory that economic factors are decisive in determining the course of history (*Spirit of Capitalism*, 1904–05). He evolved the concept of the "ideal type".

Walsh, Courtney

Welsbach, Baron Carl Auer von. (1858–1929) Austrian chemist, who patented the gas mantle (1885). His second principal invention was the alloy, the cigarette and gas-lighter flint.

Wesley, John. (1703–91) English theologian, evangelist and founder of Methodism.

Westinghouse, George. (1846–1914) American inventor and industrialist who filed more than 400 patents concerning railways, the electrical industry and the transmission of natural gas.

Wilberforce, William. (1759–1833) English philanthropist, who campaigned for the abolition of slavery.

Wingfield, Walter Clopton. (1833–1912) British inventor of lawn tennis (1874).

Witte, Count Sergei. (1849–1915) First constitutional prime minister of Russia (1905–06) who brought industrialization to Russia and promoted the Trans-Siberian Railway.

Woods, Tiger. (1975–) American golfer, who has set numerous records and is one of the world's most recognized athletes.

Woolworth, Frank Winfield. (1852–1919) American merchant, the founder of a five-and-ten-cent store from which grew the international chain of Woolworth stores.

Wren, Sir Christopher. (1632–1723) English baroque architect and professor of astronomy. He built 53 churches in London, the best known being St. Stephen Walbrook and St. James', Piccadilly. His most famous building is St. Paul's Cathedral in London.

Wright, Frank Lloyd. (1869–1959) American architect who, both structurally and formally, was perhaps the most brilliant American architect of his time.

Wright, Richard. (1908–60) American Negro novelist whose books (*Black Boy*) contain outcries against social injustice in the United States.

Wright, Wilbur. (1867–1912) **Wright, Orville.** (1871–1948) American aviation pioneers and the first men (in 1903) to fly and control a heavier-than-air machine of their own invention and construction.

Wright, Orville

Xavier, Francis. (1506–52) Navarrese Jesuit missionary and saint who could be considered the greatest Christian missionary of the Indies.

Wright, Wilbur

97

Yale, Elihu. (1649–1721) American-born Englishman in whose honour Yale University was named, in appreciation of a gift worth £560 which he sent to the young Collegiate School, then located in Connecticut.

Yamamoto, Isoroku. (1884–1943) Japanese admiral who planned the attack on Pearl Harbour in order to destroy American sea power.

Zeami, Motokiyo. (1363–1443) Japanese dramatist and actor, master of 'Noh' drama. He wrote the majority of 'Noh' plays and laid down the aesthetics of 'Noh'.

Yamamoto, Isoroku

NICKNAMES OF SOME FAMOUS PEOPLE

Boz: Charles Dickens
Coeur de Lion: Richard I of England
Edward the Peacemaker: King Edward VII of England
Farmer George: King George III of England
Lawrence of Arabia: Col. Thomas Edward Lawrence
Madonna, Our Lady of Sorrows: The Virgin Mary
Mata Hari: Marguerite Gertrude, a spy
Noll: Oliver Cromwell
Old Rough and Ready: Zachary Taylor, a president of the United States
The Apostle of the Indians: Bartholome de Las Casas
The Bard of Avon: William Shakespeare
The Beloved Disciple: St. John
The Black Napoleon: Jean Jacques Dessalines, of Haiti
The Black Prince: Son of Edward III, of England
The Blind Poet: John Milton
The Dickens of France: Honoré de Balzac
The Father of Biography: Plutarch
The Father of English Poetry: Geoffrey Chaucer
The Father of Experimental Philosophy: Francis Bacon
The Father of History: Herodotus
The Father of Medicine: Hippocrates
The Father of Modern Astronomy: Copernicus
The Father of Modern Chemistry: Antoine Lavoisier
The Father of Modern Music: Johann Sebastian Bach
The Father of Moral Philosophy: Thomas Aquinas
The Father of Natural History: John Ray

The Father of Novel Writing: Giovanni Boccaccio
The Father of Poets: Homer
The Father of the Science of Political Economy: Adam Smith
The Father of Unitarianism: John Biddle
The Faultless Painter: Andrea del Sarto
The First Gentleman in Europe: King George IV of England
The Grand Old Man: William Ewart Gladstone
The Great Commoner: William Pitt, the elder
The Inspired Idiot: Oliver Goldsmith
The Iron Chancellor, The Old Pilot: Prince Otto von Bismarck
The Iron Duke: The Duke of Wellington
The Lady of the Lamp: Florence Nightingale
The Laughing Philosopher: Democritus
The Learned Blacksmith: Elihu Burritt, an American linguist
The Light of Asia: Buddha
The Little Corporal: Napoleon Bonaparte
The Mad Monk: Rasputin
The Magnificent: Sultan Sulaiman
The Maid of Orléans: Joan of Arc
The Merrie Monarch: King Charles II of England
The Model Merchant of the Middle Ages: Richard (Dick) Whittington
The Most Musical of all Englishmen: Sir William Sterndale Bennett
The Sailor King: King William IV of England
The Scourge of God: Attila
The Sea-Green Incorruptible: Robespierre
The Seraphic Doctor: St. Bonaventura
The Swedish Nightingale: Jenny Lind
The Uncrowned Queen of Arabia: Gertrude Bell
The Wisest Fool in Christendom: King James I of England

MYTHOLOGY

Muses: Nine goddesses of the liberal arts.

Astronomy: Urania
Comedy: Thalia
Dancing: Terpsichore
Epic poetry: Calliope
History: Clio

Love poetry: Erato
Lyric poetry: Euterpe
Sacred Song: Polyhymnia
Tragedy: Melpomene

The Graces (goddesses of beauty and charm): Aglaia, Euphrosyne and Thalia.

Gods and Goddesses

God of

Day: Apollo
Dreams: Morpheus
Fertility: Priapus
Fire: Vulcan
Healing: Aesculapius
Heaven: Uranus
Herds: Apollo
Love: Cupid
Marriage: Hymen
Medicine: Apollo
Music: Apollo

Protection: Apollo
Revelry: Comus
Riches: Plutus
Rivers: Alpheus
Shepherds: Pan
Sleep: Somus
Sun: Sol, Baal
The Sea: Neptune
The Underworld: Pluto
War: Mars
Wine: Bacchus

Goddess of

Chastity: Bona Dea
Fire: Vesta
Flowers: Flora
Fruit: Pomena
Health: Hygeia
Hunting: Diana
Infatuation: Ate
Justice: Astraea
Law: Themis
Love: Venus

Morning: Aurora
Peace: Pax
Silence: Calypso
The Earth: Rhea
The Earth's Produce: Ceres
The Hearth: Vesta
Vengeance: Nemesis
War: Minerva, Bellona
Wisdom: Minerva

WEDDING ANNIVERSARIES

First: Paper
Second: Cotton
Third: Leather
Fourth: Silk
Fifth: Wood
Sixth: Iron
Seventh: Wool or copper
Eighth: Bronze
Ninth: Pottery
Tenth: Tin
Eleventh: Steel
Twelfth: Linen

Thirteenth: Lace
Fourteenth: Ivory
Fifteenth: Crystal
Twentieth: China
Twenty-fifth: Silver
Thirtieth: Pearl
Thirty-fifth: Coral or jade
Fortieth: Ruby
Forty-fifth: Sapphire
Fiftieth: Gold
Fifty-fifth: Emerald
Sixtieth: Diamond

MISCELLANEOUS

The Decalogue: The Ten Commandments
Koran: The sacred scriptures of Mohammed
Apocrypha: The fourteen books of the Old Testament. They are not included in the Authorised Version of the Bible.
Apocalypse: Book of the New Testament in which the revelation of St. John is recorded.
Canticles: The songs of Solomon.
The Major Prophets: Jeremiah, Ezekiel, Daniel, Isaiah.
Pentateuch: The first five books of the Old Testament — *Genesis, Exodus, Leviticus, Numbers, Deuteronomy.*
The Golden Rule: Do unto others as you would have others do unto you.
Gita: Hindu sacred scriptures.
The Five Senses: Seeing, hearing, feeling, smelling, tasting.
The Four Elements (ancient):   Air, fire, water, earth.
The Dead Languages: Ancient Greek and Latin.
The Three Professions: Divinity, Law, Medicine.
The Lake Poets: Coleridge, Southey, Wordsworth.
The Latin Races: French, Spanish, Portuguese, Italian.

A decade is 10 years.
A generation is about 30 years.
A century is 100 years.
A millennium is 1,000 years

Cardinal numbers are 1, 2, 3, 4, 5, etc.

Ordinal numbers are 1st, 2nd, 3rd, 4th, 5th, etc.

Cardinal points are North, South, East, West.

Cardinal signs are Aries, Libra, Cancer, Capricorn.

Cardinal virtues are prudence, temperance, justice, fortitude; or faith, hope and charity.

SOME SPECIAL DAYS

All Saints' Day: 1 March
All Souls' Day: 2 November
April Fool's Day: 1 April
Ash Wednesday: Normally held 2nd Wed. in March. However, depending on the year, it may be as early as the last week in January.

Boxing Day: 26 December

Christmas Day: 25 December
Corpus Christie Day: 30 May (Trinidad & Tobago)

Earth Day: 23 April
Emancipation Day: 1 August (Jamaica, Barbados, Trinidad & Tobago)
Errol Barrow Day: 21 January (Barbados)

Fathers' Day: 20 June

Heroes Day: 3rd Monday in October (Jamaica); 28 April (Barbados)

Independence Day: 6 August (Jamaica);
30 November (Barbados);
31 August (Trinidad & Tobago)

Kadoomente Day: 5 August (Barbados)

Mothers' Day: Second Sunday in May
Peace Day: February (Jamaica)

Shouters Day: August 31 (Trinidad & Tobago)

Teachers' Day: Second Wednesday in May (Jamaica)

Valentine's Day: 14 February

Whit Monday: 20 May (Barbados)

SEVEN WONDERS OF THE ANCIENT WORLD

The pyramids of Egypt

The hanging gardens of Babylon

The tomb of Mausolus at Halicarnassus

The temple of Diana at Ephesus

The colossus at Rhodes

The gold and ivory statue of Jupiter at Olympus

The Pharos (lighthouse) at Alexandria

ROMAN NUMERALS

I	= 1	XX	= 20
II	= 2	XXX	= 30
III	= 3	XL	= 40
IV	= 4	L	=50
V	= 5	LX	=60
VI	= 6	LXX	=70
VII	= 7	LXXX	=80
VIII	= 8	XC	=90
IX	= 9	C	=100
X	= 10	CC	=200
XI	= 11	CCC	=300
XII	= 12	CD	=400
XIII	= 13	D	=500
XIV	= 14	DC	=600
XV	= 15	DCC	=700
XVI	= 16	DCCC	=800
XVII	= 17	CM	=900
XVIII	= 18	M	=1,000
XIX	= 19	MM	=2,000

Note: A dash line over a numeral multiplies the value by 1,000.
Thus $\overline{X}$=10,000.

ABBREVIATIONS AND SYMBOLS FOR NOTE TAKING

.·. : therefore		ch.	: chapter
·.· : because		e.g.	: example
& : and		ibid.	: in the same book or passage
⊃ : implies; it follows from this that		i.e.	: that is
∃ : there is		II	: lines in a book
> : is greater than		N.B.	: note well
< : is less than		op. cit.	: in the work quoted
+ : with		p.	: page
≠ : equals, is the same as		para.	: paragraph
# : does not equal, is not the same as		pp.	: pages
= : number		Q	: question
X : character (in a novel or play)		q.v.	: for reference to this, see . . .
→ : means		v.	: versus
~ : about		viz.	: namely
c. : century		w.	: with
cf. : compare/confer		w/o.	: without

- When pressed for time vowels can be left out of a word.
- Use a dash to conclude words, e.g. test-(testing)
- Use initials for a person's name.
- Use 'n' for words ending in 'ion', e.g. conclus^n.

ARITHMETICAL FORMULAE

Rectangle

(*a*) Perimeter of rectangle = 2 (length + breadth)
$$P = 2(1+ b)$$

(*b*) Area of rectangle = length X breadth
$$A = lb$$

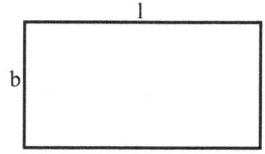

Square

(*a*) Perimeter of square = 2(length + breadth)
$$= 4a$$
$$P = 4a$$

(*b*) Area of square = length X breadth
$$A = a^2$$

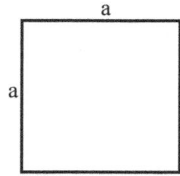

Parallelogram

Area of parallelogram = base X perpendicular height
$$A = bh$$

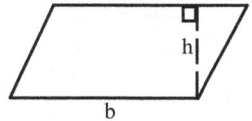

Rhombus

Area of rhombus = base X perpendicular height
$$A = bh$$

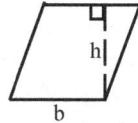

Trapezium

Area of trapezium = 1 height X sum of parallel sides
$$A = 1h(a + b)$$

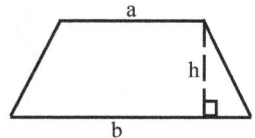

Triangle

Area of triangle = 1 baseX perpendicular height
$$A = 1bh$$

Area of triangle $=\sqrt{s(s-a)(s-b)(s-c)}$
where a, b, c, are the lengths of the three sides and
s = 1(a + b + c).
$$A = \sqrt{s(s-a)(s-b)(s-c)}$$

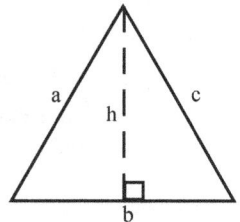

105

Right-angled Triangle

In any right-angled triangle, the square on the hypotenuse is equal to the sum of the squares on the other two sides.

$$\text{hypotenuse}^2 = \text{base}^2 + \text{height}^2$$
$$AC^2 = BC^2 + AB^2$$

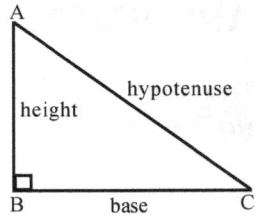

Circle

(a) Circumference of circle = 2B X radius

$$C = 2Br$$

or $C = Bd$

where d = diameter = 2r

(b) Area of circle = B (radius)^2

$$A = Br^2$$

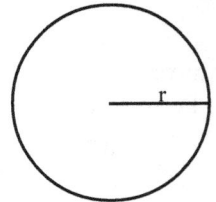

Circular Ring

Area of circular ring = $B(R + r)(R - r)$
$$A = B(R + r)(R - r)$$

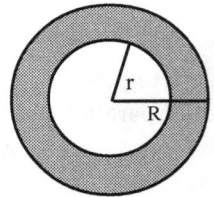

Rectangular Solid

(a) Surface area of rectangular solid
   = sum of areas of 6 faces
   = 2(lb + bh + lh)

$$A = 2(lb + bh + lh)$$

(b) Volume of rectangular solid
   = length X breadth X height

$$V = lbh$$

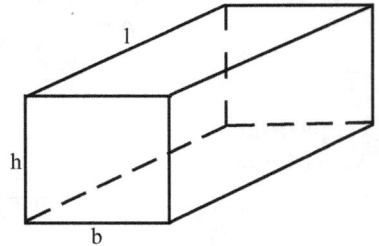

Cube

(a) Total surface area of cube
   = sum of areas of 6 faces = 6a^2

$$A = 6a^2$$

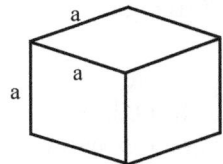

(*b*) Volume of cube = length x breadth x height

$$V = a^3$$

Cylinder
(*a*) Curved surface area of cylinder
   = circumference X length
   =2Br X 1

$$A = 2Brl$$

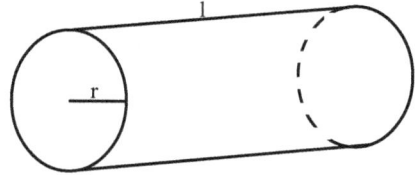

(*b*) Total surface area of cylinder
   = area of curved surface + area of both ends
   = 2Brl + 2Br²
   A = 2Brl + 2Br²

(*c*) Volume of cylinder = area of base X length
   = Br²1

$$V = Br^2 l$$

Cone
(*a*) Curved surface area of cone
   = B X radius X slant height
   = Brl

$$A = Brl$$

(*b*) Total surface area of cone
   = area of base + area of curved surface
   = Br² + Brl

$$A = Br^2 + Brl$$

(*c*) Volume of cone
   = 2 area of base X perpendicular height
   = 2Br²h

$$V = 2Br^2 h$$

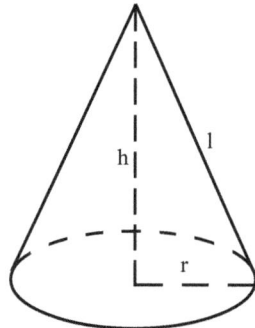

107

Sphere

(*a*) Surface area of sphere = 4Br²

$$A = 4Br^2$$

(*b*) Volume of sphere = JBr³

$$V = JBr^3$$

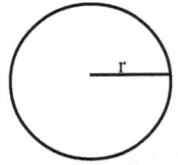

Prism

(*a*) Lateral surface area of prism
= perimeter of base X height

(*b*) Total surface area of prism
= area of lateral surface + area of both ends

(*c*) Volume of prism = area of base X height

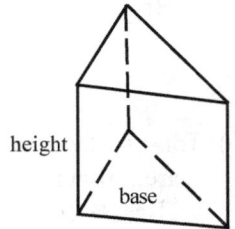

Pyramid

(*a*) Slant surface area of pyramid
= 1 perimeter of base X slant edge

(*b*) Total surface area of pyramid
= area of slant surface + area of base

(*c*) Volume of pyramid = 2 area of base X height

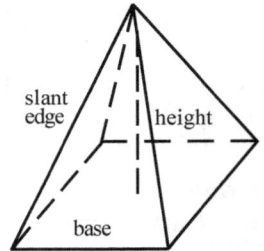

Density and Specific Gravity

(*a*) Density of a substance = $\dfrac{\text{Weight of substance}}{\text{Volume of substance}}$

(*b*) Specific gravity of a substance = $\dfrac{\text{Weight of substance}}{\text{Weight of same volume of water}}$

Simple Interest

Simple interest = $\dfrac{\text{Principal X Rate X Time}}{100}$

$$I = \frac{PRT}{100}$$

108

SI (SYSTÈME INTERNATIONAL) UNITS

	Unit	Symbol
Length	millimetre	mm
	centimetre	cm
	metre	m
	kilometre	km
Area	square centimetre	cm^2
	square metre	m^2
	square kilometre	km^2
Volume	cubic centimetre	cm^3
	cubic metre	m^3
	litre	l
Mass	gram	g
	kilogram	kg
Temperature	kelvin	K
Current	microampere	μA
	milliampere	mA
	ampere	A
Force	newton	N
Work energy	joule	J
Quantity of Heat (electrical energy)	kilowatt-hour	kWh
Power	watt	W
Voltage	volt	V
Frequency	hertz	Hz

Multiples and Sub-Multiples of SI Units

	Prefix	Symbol
10^{12}	tera	T
10^9	giga	G
10^6	mega	M
10^3	kilo	k
10^{-3}	milli	m
10^{-6}	micro	μ
10^{-9}	nano	n
10^{-12}	pica	p

Celsius and Kelvin Temperature Scales

Celsius	Kelvin
0^0C	273 K
10^0C	283 K
100^0C	373 K
-10^0C	263 K
-100^0C	173 K
-273^0C	0 K

MODERN MATHEMATICS NOTATIONS AND SYMBOLS

$E\,(U)$	:	universal set or entity
$\cup$	:	union of sets
$\cap$	:	intersection of sets
$\subset$	:	is a subset of or "included in" or "contained in"
$\not\subset$	:	is not a subset of
$\in$	:	is a member or an element of
$\notin$	:	is not a member of
$\{\ \}$ or $\emptyset$	:	null set or an empty set
$n(P)$	:	number of members in set P
P'	:	complement of set P
$\Rightarrow$	:	implies
$\Leftarrow$	:	is implied by
$\Leftrightarrow$	:	implies and is implied by or is equivalent to
$>$	:	is greater than
$<$	:	is less than
$\geqslant$	:	is greater than and equal to
$\leqslant$	:	is less than and equal to
$\leftrightarrow$	:	one to one correspondence
$\div$	:	is approximately equal to
$\neq$	:	is not equal to
$(a,\,b)$	:	ordered pair $a,\,b$
$\begin{pmatrix} a \\ b \end{pmatrix}$	:	ordered pair $a,\,b$ representing a vector
v(AB) or $\overrightarrow{AB}$	:	vector AB or displacement AB
AB	:	line segment AB
m(AB)	:	measure or length of line segment AB
+ve	:	positive
–ve	:	negative
R	:	set of real numbers
Q	:	set of rational numbers
Z	:	set of integers $\{...\,-3,\,-2,\,-1,\,0,\,1,\,2,\,3,\,..............\}$
W	:	set of whole numbers $\{0,\,1,\,2,\,3,\,..............\}$
N	:	set of natural numbers $\{1,\,2,\,3,\,4,\,..............\}$

The set of prime numbers $\{2,\,3,\,5,\,7,\,..............\}$

The set of composite numbers $\{1,\,4,\,6,\,8,\,9,\,..............\}$

The set of irrational numbers $\{...\ \sqrt{2},\ \dfrac{\sqrt{2}}{3},\ \dfrac{\sqrt{2}}{5},\ \dfrac{\sqrt{7}}{3},\ ....\}$

PROOF-READING SYMBOLS

∧	Make correction indicated in margin.	*W.f.*	Wrong font; change to proper font.
.... *Stet*	Retain words under which dots appear; write 'Stet' in margin.	*l.c.*	Put in lower case (small letters)
×	Appears battered; examine.	*s.c.*	Put in small capitals
≡	Straighten lines.	*Caps*	Put in capitals
✓✓✓	Unevenly spaced; correct spacing.	*C. + s.c.*	Put in caps and small caps.
//	Line up; i.e., make lines even with other matter.	*rom.*	Change to Roman.
run on	Make no break in the reading; no ¶.	*ital*	Change to italic.
out see copy	Here is an omission; see copy.	≡	Under letter or word means caps.
¶	Make a paragraph here.	=	Under letter or word means small caps.
trs	Transpose words or letters as indicated.	—	Under letter or word means Italic.
/	Take out matter indicated; delete.	⌄⌄⌄	Under letter or word means bold face.
⌀	Take out character indicated; and close up.	,/	Insert comma.
¢	Line drawn through a cap means lower case.	;/	Insert semicolon.
⊙	Upside down; reverse.	:/	Insert colon.
○	Close up; no space.	⊙	Insert period.
#	Insert a space here.	/?/	Insert interrogation mark.
⌐	Push down this space.	(!)	Insert exclamation mark.
□	Indent line one em.	/=/	Insert hypen.
⌐	Move this to the left.	✓/	Insert apostrophe.
⌐	Move this to the right.	⌄/ ⌄/	Insert quotation marks.
⌐	Raise to proper position.	✓	Insert superior letter or figure.
⌐	Lower to proper position.	⌐	Insert inferior letter or figure.
////	Hair space letters	[/]	Insert brackets.
		(/)	Insert parenthesis.
		—	One-em dash.

111

WEIGHTS AND MEASURES

IMPERIAL SYSTEM

LINEAL

12 inches	= 1 foot
3 feet	= 1 yard
$5\frac{1}{2}$ yards	= 1 rod, pole or perch
4 poles	= 1 chain
10 chains	= furlong
8 furlongs or 1,760 yards	= 1 mile

AREA

144 sq inches	= 1 sq foot
9 sq feet	= 1 sq yard
$30\frac{1}{4}$ sq yards	= 1 sq pole, rod or perch
40 sq poles	= 1 rood
4 roods	= 1 acre
640 acres	= 1 sq mile

VOLUME

1,728 cu inches	= 1 cu foot
27 cu feet	= 1 cu yard

AVOIRDUPOIS WEIGHT

16 drams	= 1 ounce (oz)
16 ounces	= 1 pound (lb)
14 pounds	= 1 stone
28 pounds	= 1 quarter
100 pounds	= 1 cental
4 quarters	= 1 hundredweight
8 stones	= 1 hundredweight (cwt)
20 hundredweights	= 1 ton

CAPACITY (Dry)

8.4 cu inches	= 1 gill
4 gills	= 1 pint
2 pints	= 1 quart
4 quarts	= 1 gallon
2 gallons	= 1 peck
4 pecks	= 1 bushel
8 bushels	= 1 quarter

CAPACITY (Liquid)

4 gills	= 1 pint
2 pints	= 1 quart
4 quarts	= 1 gallon
$31\frac{1}{2}$ gallons	= 1 barrel
2 barrels	= 1 hogshead

METRIC SYSTEM

LINEAL

1,000 microns	= 1 millimetre
10 millimetres	= 1 centimetre
10 centimetres	= 1 decimetre
100 centimetres	= 1 metre
10 metres	= 1 decametre
100 metres	= 1 hectometre
1,000 metres	= 1 kilometre
10 kilometres	= 1 myriametre

WEIGHT

10 grams	= 1 dekagram
100 grams	= 1 hectogram
1,000 grams	= 1 kilogram
10 kilograms	= 1 myriagram
50 kilograms	= 1 centner
100 kilograms	= 1 quintal
1,000 kilograms	= 1 tonne

AREA

100 sq centimetres	= 1 sq decimetre
100 sq decimetres	= 1 sq metre
100 sq metres	= 1 area
100 ares	= 1 hectare
100 hectares	= 1 sq kilometre
100 sq kilometres	= 1 sq myriametre

VOLUME

1,000 cu centimetres	= 1 cu decimetre
1,000 cu decimetres	= 1 cu metre

CAPACITY

10 centilitres	= 1 decilitre
10 decilitre	= 1 litre
10 litres	= 1 decalitre
100 litres	= 1 hectolitre

112

IMPERIAL—METRIC

LINEAL
1 inch	= 25.39998 millimetres
1 foot	= 0.30479 metre
1 yard	= 0.914399 metre
1 mile	= 1.609343 kilometres

AREA
1 sq inch	= 6.45163 sq centimetres
1 sq foot	= 0.9290 sq metre
1 acre	= 0.40469 hectare
1 sq mile	= 2.59000 sq kilometres

VOLUME
1 cu inch	= 16.386993 cu centimetres
1 cu foot	= 0.02832 cu metre

CAPACITY
1 pint	= 0.56795 litre
1 gallon	= 4.54609 litres

WEIGHT
1 ounce	= 28.349530 grams
1 pound	= 0.453592 kilogram
1 cwt	= 50.80234 kilograms
1 ton	= 1,016.0470 kilograms

METRIC—IMPERIAL

1 millimetre	=	0.039370 inch
1 metre	=	3.28091 feet
1 metre	=	1.093614 yards
1 kilometre	=	0.621372 mile

1 sq centimetre	=	0.15500 sq inch
1 sq metre	=	10.76387 sq feet
1 hectare	=	2.47104 acres
1 sq kilometre	=	0.38610 sq mile

1 cu centimetre	=	0.061024 cu inch
1 cu metre	=	35.31445 cu feet

1 litre	=	1.76072 pints
1 litre	=	0.22009 gallon

1 gram	=	0.035270 ounce
1 kilogram	=	2.204620 pounds
1 kilogram	=	0.01968 cwt
1 kilogram	=	0.000984 ton

TEMPERATURE

FREEZING AND BOILING POINTS

Fahrenheit — Freezing Point, 32°
      Boiling Point, 212°

Celsius   — Freezing Point, 0°
      Boiling Point, 100°

THERMOMETRICAL CONVERSION FORMULAE

Celsius to Fahrenheit = (Celsius × 1.8) + 32
Fahrenheit to Celsius = (Fahrenheit − 32) × 0.555

SECTION THREE
GEOGRAPHY

GEOGRAPHIC TERMS

Acclimatize. To become accustomed to a new climate.

Air. The mixture of invisible, tasteless and odourless gases surrounding the earth.

Alluvium. Material such as mud, sand, silt and gravel, carried in suspension and deposited by a river.

Altimeter. An instrument used to indicate height above sea level.

Antarctic. The region around the South Pole.

Arch. An opening through a mass of rocks.

Arctic. The north polar region.

Arctic Circle. The $66^0 32'$N latitude, lying between the North Frigid and North Temperate zones.

Arid climate. A dry climate, especially of deserts.

Atoll. A ring-like coral reef.

Autumn. A season of the year.

Avalanche. Descent of material down a mountain slope, usually used in reference to snow and ice.

Axis. Imaginary line passing through the centre of the earth and joining the North and South Poles.

Barometer. An instrument for measuring atmospheric pressure.

Barrel. Liquid measure used in the petroleum industry which is equivalent to 159 litres (35 imperial gallons).

Barysphere. The earth's core and mantle.

Basin. A term loosely applied to a natural or artificial indentation in the earth's crust.

Bathymetry. The measurement of the depth of the ocean, sea or lake.

Bay. A wide, curved inlet of a sea or lake.

Biosphere. A term in ecology which refers to the part of the earth which supports life.

Boulder. A large detached piece of rock.

Bronze Age. Historical period between the Stone and Iron Ages.

Built-up area. The part of a town covered with buildings.

Cainozoic. The most recent geological era, beginning about 65 million years ago.

Calabash. The gourd that grows on the tropical vine *Lagenaria siceraria*.

Calm. Absence of any wind.

Canal. An artificial waterway.

Cancer, Tropic of. The northern tropic at latitude 23^0 32'N.

Canyon. A steep-walled gorge, usually having a river.

Cape. A headland or promontory projecting into the sea or a lake.

Capricorn, Tropic of. The southern tropic at latitude 23^0 32'S.

Carat. A measure of weight for precious stones.

Cardinal points. The four main directions of the compass — North, East, South and West.

Cash crop. A crop cultivated for sale.

Cassava (manioc). A tropical plant. Tapioca is a granular form of cassava.

Cassiterite. The most important tin-bearing ore.

Cave. An underground hollow usually accessible from the surface.

Chinook. A warm, dry westerly wind blowing down the eastern slopes of the Rockies.

Climate. Weather conditions of a region over a long period.

Cloud. A floating mass of minute water droplets.

Col. A pass in a ridge.

Collective farming. A farming system in which small holdings are formed into a single large unit under government supervision.

Compass. An instrument to determine direction.

Condensation. The changing of water from gas to liquid or solid.

Continent. A large, unbroken land mass.

Corrosion: The wearing away of rocks by a chemical process.

Current. The flow of air or water in a certain direction.

Cybernetics. The study of communication and control in machines and living organisms.

Cyclone. A small, intense low-pressure system and an associated revolving storm accompanied by rain. It is also known as a hurricane.

Dam. A barrier created to hold and store water.

Delta. A flat area of alluvium at the mouth of a river.

Desalination. The removal of salt from sea water to produce fresh water.

Desert. An area with little rainfall and vegetation.

Dew. A deposit of water droplets on objects near the ground.

Drought. A period of dry weather.

Dune. A ridge of sand shaped by the wind.

Earthquake. A violent tremor in the earth's crust, sending out shock waves in all directions.

Eclipse. A partial or total obstruction of the light of one planet by another planet.

Ecology. The study of living organisms in relation to their environment.

Equator. The greater circle around the earth separating the northern and southern hemispheres.

Equinox. The time of the year when the sun is directly overhead at the equator at midday. There are two equinoxes; the spring, or vernal, and the autumnal.

Estuary. The mouth of a river, where fresh and sea water mix.

Evaporation. The process by which a liquid changes directly into vapour or gas.

Fathom. A unit of measure for ocean depth. 1 fathom = 1.8 m = 6 feet.

Fauna. The animal life of a region.

Fog. A ground-level cloud that severely reduces visibility.

Forecast. A prediction of weather conditions.

Forest. A large, uncultivated area of dense trees.

Frontier. A stretch of land bordering another country.

Frost. The weather condition when water vapour freezes.

Gale. The common term for a high-velocity wind.

Gap. A natural break in a ridge.

Geography. The study of the features of the earth's surface, such as relief, climate, vegetation, soils and economic resources.

Geyser. Intermittent, forceful gush of hot water from a reservoir in the ground.

Gradient. The steepness of a slope.

Harbour. A sheltered place where ships can anchor.

Heat wave. A spell of abnormally hot weather.

Horizon. The line where the earth and sky appear to meet.

Humidity. The degree of dampness of the air and one of the main influences on weather.

Hurricane. A cyclonic storm experienced in the Gulf of Mexico and the West Indies.

Hydration. The addition of water to minerals which do not contain water in their crystals.

Hydroelectricity. The generation of electricity by falling water.

Ice. The solid state of water cooled below its freezing point.

Inlet. A narrow opening of the sea or lake into the land.

International Date Line.   An imaginary line following approximately the 180°
meridian in the Pacific Ocean.   When crossing the line from east to west, one
day is added; from west to east one day is subtracted.
Iso-.   Prefix used to denote lines of equal value on maps.
Isthmus.   An extremely narrow stretch of land joining two larger land areas.

Jungle.   A dense tropical forest.

Karoo.   A natural region of South Africa between the coastlands and plateau.
Khamsin.   A warm, dry southerly wind blowing over Egypt.

Lagoon.   A shallow body of water separated from the sea by a strip of land.
Lake.   A body of water occupying a hollow in the earth's surface.
Landform.   A topographic feature of the earth's surface.
Latitude.   An angular distance on the earth's surface north or south of the
equator.
Lava.   Molten material from the earth's interior extruded during a volcanic
eruption.
Longitude.   Angular distance measured in degrees, from 0° to 180° , east or
west of the Greenwich meridian.

Mangrove.   Common name for tropical plants growing in bays, lagoons and
rivers.
Map.   A scaled drawing of the earth, or portion of it, represented on paper.
Marsh.   An area of soft, wet land, usually treeless.
Meridian.   A semicircle passing from the North to the South Pole.
Meteorite.   A mass of hard matter from outer space.
Midnight sun.   Phenomenon which occurs only within the Arctic and Antarctic
circles in midsummer, when the sun does not sink below the horizon.
Mirage.   An optical illusion caused by the refraction of light through a layer of
hot air.
Mist.   A mass of minute water droplets forming a veil at ground level.
Mistral.   A cold, dry north-western wind blowing in winter from the Central
Massif in France down the Rhone Valley.
Monoculture.   The cultivation of only one crop e.g. wheatlands of the Cana-
dian prairies, rice fields of Burma.
Monsoon.   Seasonal winds accompanied by torrential rains.
Moon.   The only satellite of the earth. The moon is one-quarter the size of the
earth.
Moor.   Uncultivated, wild tract of land, usually hilly.
Mountain.   A landform at a higher elevation than the surrounding land.

117

Nevados. Cold Andean winds blowing down the elevated valleys of Ecuador.

Nimbus. A cloud from which rain falls.

Norther. Dry cold wind which sweeps down the middle of North America towards Texas and the Gulf Coast states during winter.

Oasis. An area in a desert where water is found.

Ocean. The great mass of salt water surrounding the continents. Seventy per cent of the earth's surface is covered by ocean.

Oceanography. The scientific study of the oceans of the earth.

Opisometer. A device for measuring distance on a map.

Pampas. A vast, low-lying expanse of temperate grassland in Argentina and Uruguay.

Panhandle. A narrow strip of a territory or state projecting into another.

Pantograph. An instrument for enlarging or reducing maps.

Papagayo. A cold, violent northerly wind blowing along the coastal areas of Mexico and Central America.

Pass. A gap in a mountain range.

Pasture. A tract of grassland used for grazing animals.

Peak. A mountain with a pointed top.

Peninsula. A stretch of long, narrow land projecting into a sea or lake.

Piedmont. The area at the foot of a mountain.

Plain. A flat stretch of land of low elevation.

Plateau. An upland area with steep slopes and a level summit.

Prairie. A stretch of undulating land covered with grasses.

Precipice. A vertical rock face of considerable height.

Quagmire. A bog or soft, wet ground.

Quicksand. A mass of loose sand with water.

Race. One of the principal divisions of mankind.

Range. A line or chain of mountains.

Rapid. A part of a river where the current flows fast.

Ravine. A narrow, steep-sided valley formed by running water.

Reef. A strip of coral or rock lying close to the surface of the sea or rising above it.

Relief. The variations in height between high and low points on the earth's surface.

Reservoir. An area for storing water for domestic or industrial use.

Richter scale. The scale used to measure the magnitude of earthquakes.

Rock. The hard material forming part of the earth's crust, usually composed of several minerals.

Savannah.   An expanse of tropical grassland between equatorial forests and hot deserts.

Scrub.   A type of vegetation, consisting of grasses, bushes and stunted trees.

Season.   A period of the year characterised by a set of climatic conditions. There are four seasons: spring, summer, autumn, winter.

Seaway.   An ocean shipping route.

Sirocco.   A hot wind blowing from the Sahara across North Africa and southern Italy.

Smallholding.   A small cultivated plot of land.

Smog.   Fog that has been polluted by smoke, dust, carbon monoxide and sulphur dioxide.

Snow.   Rain in the form of minute crystals, occurring when the temperatures fall below 0^0 C.

Soil.   The material on the earth's surface, made up of solid, liquid and gaseous substances.

Solstice.   The time of the year in summer or winter when the sun reaches its maximum angular distance from the equator.

Sounding.   A method used to find out the depth of water.

Spa.   A medicinal spring usually developed as a health resort.

Spate.   A sudden river flood caused by heavy rainfall.

Spring.   Water issuing naturally from the ground.

Squall.   A violent wind accompanied by rainfall, lasting only for a short period.

Stalactite.   Calcium carbonate suspended vertically from the roof of a limestone cave.

Stalagmite.   Calcium carbonate which builds upwards from the floor of a limestone cave.

Steppe.   The natural grasslands stretching from south-eastern Europe to central Asia.

Storm.   A high wind accompanied by rain, snow, hail or sleet, thunder and lightning.

Subsidence.   The sinking of a section of the earth's crust.

Subtropical.   A term describing the areas of the earth lying between the Tropic of Cancer and 35^0N and between the Tropic of Capricorn and 35^0S.

Temperate zone.   A climatic zone between the frigid (polar) and torrid (tropical) zones.

Temperature.   The degree of heat or cold measured by a thermometer.

Terracing.   Cutting steps on a hillside for the cultivation of crops.

Thaw.   The change from snow or ice to water.

Thermal.   Pertaining to heat or temperature.

Tide.   The rise and fall of ocean water level, caused by the pull of the moon and the sun.

Topography. The description or representation on a map of the surface features of an area.

Tornado. A whirlwind accompanied by a funnel-shaped cloud, heavy rain and thunder.

Torrid zone. The tropical belt lying on both sides of the equator.

Town. A compact, urban settlement.

Trade winds. Winds blowing from subtropical belts towards the equatorial low-pressure region.

Transit trade. Trade between two countries that passes through a third country.

Tremor. An earthquake of low intensity.

Tundra. A treeless arctic or subarctic plain lying across the extreme north of North America.

Urban. Pertaining to a city or town.

Valley. A linear depression on a land surface, often containing a river.

Vegetation. The collective term for the plant life or flora of an area.

Veld. A tract of open grassland in South Africa.

Volcano. A cone-shaped formation of lava, emitted under pressure from the earth's interior.

Waterway. A navigable channel.

Weather. The atmospheric conditions prevailing at a specific time.

Whirlpool. A circular motion of water in the sea.

Wind. The natural movement of air over the earth's surface.

Zone. A term denoting an area within which similar characteristics prevail.

COUNTRIES AND THEIR CAPITALS

Country	Capital
Afghanistan	Kabul
Albania	Tiranë
Algeria	Algiers
Andorra	Andorra la Vella
Angola	Luanda
Argentina	Buenos Aires
Armenia	Yerevan
Australia	Canberra
Austria	Vienna
Azerbaijan	Baku
Bahamas	Nassau
Bahrain	Manama
Bangladesh	Dhaka
Belarus	Minsk
Belgium	Brussels
Belize	Belmopan
Benin	Porto Novo
Bermuda	Hamilton
Bhutan	Thimphu
Bolivia	La Paz / Sucre
Bosnia &	Sarajevo
Herzegovinia	
Botswana	Gaborone
Brazil	Brasilia
Bulgaria	Sofia
Burkina Faso	Ouagadougou
Burundi	Bujumbura
Cambodia	Phnom Penh
Cameroon	Yaoundé
Canada	Ottawa
Cape Verde	Praia
Central African	Bangui
Republic	
Chad	Ndjamena
Chile	Santiago
China (People's	Peking
Republic of)	
Colombia	Bogotá

Country	Capital
Comoros	Moroni
Congo	Brazzaville
Congo (Zaire)	Kinshasa
Costa Rica	San José
Croatia	Zagreb
Cyprus	Nicosia
Czech Republic	Prague
Denmark	Copenhagen
Djibouti	Djibouti
Ecuador	Quito
Egypt	Cairo
El Salvador	San Salvador
Equatorial	Malabo
Eritrea	Asmara
Ethiopia	Addis Ababa
Estonia	Tallinn
Fiji	Suva
Finland	Helsinki
France	Paris
Gabon	Libreville
Gambia	Banjul
Georgia	Tbilisi
Germany	Berlin
Ghana	Accra
Greece	Athens
Greenland	Nuuk
	(Godthaab)
Guatemala	Guatemala
	City
Guinea	Conakry
Guinea-Bissau	Bissau
Guyana	Georgetown
Honduras	Tegucigalpa
Hong Kong	Victoria

121

Country	Capital
Hungary	Budapest
Iceland	Reykjavík
India	New Delhi
Indonesia	Jakarta
Iran	Tehran
Iraq	Bagdad
Ireland (Republic of)	Dublin
Israel	Jerusalem
Italy	Rome
Ivory Coast	Yamoussouko
Japan	Tokyo
Jordan	Amman
Kazakhstan	Akmola
Kenya	Nairobi
Kiribati	Bairiki
Korea, North	Pyongyang
Korea, South	Seoul
Kuwait	Kuwait
Laos	Vientiane
Latvia	Riga
Lebanon	Beirut
Lesotho	Maseru
Liberia	Monrovia
Libya	Tripoli
Liechtenstein	Vaduz
Lithuania	Vilnius
Luxembourg	Luxembourg
Macedonia	Skopje
Madagascar	Atananarive
Malawi	Lilongwe
Malaysia	Kaula Lumpur
Maldives	Male
Mali	Bamako
Malta	Valletta
Marshall Islands	Majuro

Country	Capital
Mauritania	Nouakchott
Mauritius	Port Louis
Mexico	Mexico City
Micronesia	Palikir
Moldova	Chisinau
Monaco	Monaco
Mongolia	Ulan Bator
Morocco	Rabat
Mozambique	Maputo
Myanmar	Rangoon
Nauru	Uaboe
Nepal	Katmandu
Netherlands (Holland)	Amsterdam
New Zealand	Wellington
Nicaragua	Managua
Niger	Niamey
Nigeria	Abuja
Norway	Oslo
Oman	Muscat
Pakistan	Islamabad
Palau	Oreor
Panama	Panama City
Papua New Guinea	Port Moresby
Paraguay	Asunción
Peru	Lima
Philippines	Manila
Poland	Warsaw
Portugal	Lisbon
Qatar	Doha
Rumania/Romania	Bucharest
Russia (formerly (U.S.S.R.)	Moscow
Rwanda	Kigali
Samoa	Apia

Country	Capital	Country	Capital
San Marino	San Marino	Togo	Lomé
São Tomé-Príncipe	São Tomé	Tonga	Nukualofa
Saudi Arabia	Riyadh	Tunisia	Tunis
Senegal	Dakar	Turkey	Ankara
Seychelles	Victoria	Tuvalu	Fongafale
Sierra Leone	Freetown		
Singapore	Singapore	Uganda	Kampala
Slovakia	Bratislava	Ukraine	Kiev
Slovenia	Ljubljana	United Arab Emirates	Abu Dhabi
Solomon Islands	Honiara	United Kingdom	London
Somalia	Mogadishu	United States of America	Washington, D.C.
South Africa (Republic of)	Pretoria	Uruguay	Montevideo
Spain	Madrid	Uzbekistan	Tashkent
Sri Lanka	Colombo		
Sudan	Khartoum	Vanuatu	Port-Vila
Surinam	Paramaribo	Venezuela	Caracas
Swaziland	Mbabane	Vietnam	Hanoi
Sweden	Stockholm		
Switzerland	Bern	Western Samoa	Apia
Syria	Damascus		
		Yemen	Sanaa
Taiwan (Republic of China)	Taipei	Yugoslavia	Belgrade
Tajikistan	Dushanbe	Zambia	Lusaka
Turkmenistan	Ashgabat	Zimbabwe	Harare
Tanzania	Dodoma		
Thailand	Bangkok		

Country	Capital

CARIBBEAN COUNTRIES AND THEIR CAPITALS

Country	Capital	Country	Capital
Anguilla	The Valley	Bermuda	Hamilton
Antigua	St. John's		
Barbados	Bridgetown	Cayman Islands	Georgetown
Barbuda	Codrington	Cuba	Havana

Country	Capital	Country	Capital
Dominica	Roseau	Netherlands Antilles	Willemstad
Dominican Republic	Santo Domingo	Puerto Rico	San Juan
Grenada	St. George's	St. Lucia	Castries
Guadeloupe	Basse-Terre	St. Vincent	Kingstown
Guyana	Georgetown	Trinidad and Tobago	Port of Spain
Jamaica	Kingston	Virgin Islands (British)	Road Town
Martinique	Forte-de-France	Virgin Islands (USA)	Charlotte Amalie
Montserrat	Plymouth		

NICKNAMES OF SOME COUNTRIES AND CITIES

Africa: *The Dark Continent*
Algeria, Libya, Morocco, Tunisia: *The Barbary States*
Andalusia: *The Granary of Spain*
Arizona: *The Copper State*
Athens: *The Eye of Greece*
Australasia: *The Land of Eucalyptus*
Australia: *The Land of the Golden Fleece*
Azores: *The Island of the Hawks*

Baghdad: *The City of the Arabian Nights*
Balkans: *The Cockpit of Europe*
Belgium: *The Battlefield of Europe*
Benares: *The Holy City of the Hindus*
Boston: *The Hub of the Universe*
British Columbia: *The Sea of Mountains*
Bucharest: *The Paris of the East; City of Pleasure*
Budapest: *The Twin City*

California: *The Golden State*
Canada: *Our Lady of Snow*
Chicago: *Windy City*

China: *The Celestial Empire; The Land of Han*
Cincinnati: *Queen City*
Connecticut: *The Nutmeg State*
Costa Rica: *Rich Coast*

Damascus: *The Pearl of the Orient*
Delaware: *The Blue Hen State*
Denmark: *The Dairy of Northern Europe*
Detroit: *The Automobile Capital of the World*

Edinburgh: *The Athens of the North*
Egypt: *The Gift of the Nile*

Finland: *The Land of a Thousand Lakes*

Germany: *The Fatherland*
Gothland: *The Eye of the Baltic*
Guyana: *The Magnificient Province*

Hawaii: *The Halfway House of the Pacific*

Ireland: *The Emerald Isle*

Japan: *The Land of the Rising Sun*
Jerusalem: *The Holy City*
Johannesburg: *The Golden City*

Kent (County): *The Garden of England*
Kentucky: *The Blue Grass State*
Kiev: *The Mother City of Russia*
Kimberley: *The Diamond City*

Lancashire (County): *County Palatine*
Le Havre: *The Liverpool of France*
Liege: *The Birmingham of Belgium*

Mexico: *The Storehouse of the World*
Minneapolis and St. Paul: *The Twin Cities of the Mississippi*

Netherlands (Holland): *The Land of Tulips; The Land of Dykes*
Nevada: *The Silver State*

New Haven: *City of Elms*
New Jersey: *The Garden State*
New Zealand: *The Antipodes*
Norway: *The Land of the Midnight Sun*

Punjab (in Pakistan and India): *The Land of the Five Rivers*

Rome: *The Eternal City*

Scotland: *Caledonia; The Land of Oat Cakes*
Sweden: *The Sawmill of Europe*
Switzerland: *The Playground of Europe*

Thailand: *The Land of the White Elephant*
Thebes: *Valley of Kings*
Tibet: *The Roof of the World*

Venezuela: *Little Venice*
Virginia: *The Old Dominion*

Washington D.C.: *The City of Magnificent Distances*

NICKNAMES OF SOME CARIBBEAN ISLANDS

Barbados: *The Land of the Flying Fish*
Cuba: *The Pearl of the Antilles; The Sugar-mill of the Antilles*
Grenada: *The Spice Island of the West*
Haiti: *Mountainous Country*
Jamaica: *Land of Wood and Water; The Isle of Springs*
Puerto Rico: *Rich Port*
Tobago: *Robinson Crusoe's Island*
Trinidad: *The Land of the Hummingbird*

CURRENCIES OF THE WORLD

Country	Currency
Afghanistan	afghani
Albania	lek
Algeria	dinar
Andorra	euro
Argentina	peso
Armenia	dram
Australia	dollar
Austria	euro
Azerbaijan	manat
Bahrain	dinar
Bangladesh	taka
Barbados	dollar
Belarus	rouble
Belgium	euro
Benin	CFA franc
Bhutan	Ngultrum
Bolivia	boliviano
Bosnia & Herzegovinia	marks
Botswana	pula
Brazil	real
Bulgaria	lev
Burkina Faso	CFA franc
Burundi	franc
Cambodia	riel
Cameroon	CFA franc
Canada	dollar
Central African Republic	CFA franc
Chad	CFA franc
Chile	peso
China	yuan
Columbia	peso
Congo	CFA franc
Costa Rica	colón
Croatia	kuna
Cuba	peso
Cyprus	pound
Czech Republic	koruna

Country	Currency
Denmark	krone
Dominican Republic	peso
Ecuador	US dollar
Egypt	pound
El Salvador	colón
Equatorial Guinea	CFA franc
Eritrea	nakfa
Estonia	kroon
Ethiopia	birr
Fiji	dollar
Finland	euro
France	euro
Gabon	CFA franc
Gambia	dalasi
Georgia	lari
Germany	euro
Ghana	cedi
Greece	euro
Guatemala	quetzal
Guinea	franc
Guyana	dollar
Haiti	gourde
Honduras	lempira
Hungary	forint
Iceland	krona
India	rupee
Indonesia	rupiah
Iran	rial
Iraq	dinar
Ireland	euro
Israel	new shekel
Italy	euro
Ivory Coast	CFA franc
Jamaica	dollar

127

Country	Currency
Japan	yen
Jordan	dinar
Kazakhstan	tenge
Kenya	shilling
Kiribati	Australian dollar
Korea	won
Kuwait	dinar
Laos	kip
Latvia	lats
Lebanon	pound
Lesotho	loti
Liberia	dollar
Libya	dinar
Liechtenstein	Swiss franc
Lithuania	litus
Luxembourg	euro
Macedonia	denar
Madagascar	franc
Malawi	kwacha
Malaysia	ringgit
Maldives	rufiyaa
Mali	CFA franc
Malta	lira
Marshall Islands	US dollar
Mauritania	ouguiya
Mauritius	rupee
Mexico	peso
Micronesia	US dollar
Moldova	leu
Monaco	euro
Mongolia	tughrik
Morocco	dirham
Myanmar	kyat
Nauru	dollar
Nepal	rupee
Netherlands	euro
New Zealand	dollar
Nicaragua	córdoba
Niger	CFA franc

Country	Currency
Nigeria	naira
Norway	krone
Oman	rial
Pakistan	rupee
Palau	US dollar
Panama	balboa
Paraguay	guarani
Peru	nuevo sol
Philippines	peso
Poland	zloty
Portugal	euro
Qatar	riyal
Romania	leu
Russia	rouble
Rwanda	franc
Samoa	tala
San Marino	euro
Saudi Arabia	riyal
Senegal	CFA franc
Sierra Leone	leone
Singapore	dollar
Solomon Islands	dollar
Solvakia	koruna
Slovenia	tolar
Somalia	shilling
South Africa	euro
Spain	euro
Sri Lanka	rupee
Sudan	dinar
Swaziland	lilangeni
Sweden	krona
Switzerland	franc
Syria	pound
Taiwan	dollar
Tajikistan	somoni
Tanzania	shilling
Thailand	baht

Country	Currency
Togo	CFA franc
Tonga	pa'anga
Trinidad and Tobago	dollar
Tunisia	dinar
Tuvalu	Australian dollar
Turkmenistan	manat
Turkey	lira
Uganda	shilling
Ukraine	hryvnia
United Arab Emirates	dirham

Country	Currency
United Kingdom	pound
United States	US dollar
Uruguay	peso
Uzbekistan	sum
Vanuatu	vatu
Venezuela	bolívar
Vietnam	dong
Yugoslavia	dinar
Zambia	kwacha
Zimbabwe	dollar

129

MISCELLANEOUS

CONTINENTS OF THE WORLD

Name	Area ('000)		Population
Asia	43,999 sq km	(16,988 sq mi)	3,674,000,000
Africa	29,800 sq km	(11,506 sq mi)	778,000,000
North America	24,320 sq km	(9,390 sq mi)	483,000,000
South America	17,599 sq km	(6,795 sq mi)	342,000,000
Antarctica	14,245 sq km	(5,500 sq mi)	—
Europe	9,700 sq km	(3,745 sq mi)	732,653,000
Australia	7,687 sq km	(2,968 sq mi)	31,000,000

MAJOR OCEAN DEEPS OF THE WORLD

Name	Ocean	Locality	Depth
Vityaz	West Pacific	Mariana Trench	10,859 m (36,198 ft)
Challenger	West Pacific	Mariana Trench	10,692 m (35,640 ft)
Kermadec	South Pacific	Kermadec Trench	10,634 m (35,445 ft)
Tonga	South Pacific	Tonga Trench	10,602 m (35,341 ft)
Horizon	South Pacific	Tonga Trench	10,465 m (34,884 ft)
Cape Johnson	West Pacific	Philippine Trench	10,331 m (34,438 ft)
Emden	West Pacific	Philippine Trench	10,236 m (34,120 ft)

OCEANS AND SEAS OF THE WORLD

Name	Area('000)	Location
Pacific Ocean	166,242 sq km (64,186 sq mi)	
Atlantic Ocean	85,506 sq km (33,400 sq mi)	
Indian Ocean	73,427 sq km (28,350 sq mi)	
Arctic Ocean	13,222 sq km (5,105 sq mi)	
South China Sea	2,973 sq km (1,148 sq mi)	Part of West Pacific, off the coasts of S.E. Asia
Caribbean Sea	2,515 sq km (971 sq mi)	Between Central America, West Indies and South America

Name	Area ('000)	Location
Mediterranean Sea	2,510 sq km (969 sq mi)	Between Europe, Africa and Asia
Bering Sea	2,261 sq km (873 sq mi)	Part of North Pacific between northern North America and northern Asia
Gulf of Mexico	1,507 sq km (582 sq mi)	Arm of North Atlantic, off south-east coast of North America
Sea of Okhotsk	1,391 sq km (537 sq mi)	Arm of North Pacific, off north-east coast of Asia
Sea of Japan	1,013 sq km (391 sq mi)	Arm of North Pacific between Asian mainland and Japan
Hudson Bay	730 sq km (282 sq mi)	Northern North America
East China Sea	663 sq km (256 sq mi)	Part of North Pacific, off the east coast of Asia
Andaman Sea	565 sq km (218 sq mi)	Off the south coast of Asia
Black Sea	508 sq km (196 sq mi)	Between S.E. Europe and West Asia
Red Sea	453 sq km (175 sq mi)	Arm of the Indian Ocean between North Africa and the Arabian Peninsula
North Sea	427 sq km (165 sq mi)	Off the coast of N.W. Europe
Yellow Sea	293 sq km (113 sq mi)	Part of North Pacific, off the east coast of Asia

MAJOR WATERFALLS OF THE WORLD

Name	Location	Height
Angel	Venezuela	964 m (3,212 ft)
Tugela	South Africa	933 m (3,110 ft)
Yosemite	Calif., U.S.A.	728 m (2,425 ft)
Cuquenan	Venezuela	600 m (2,000 ft)
Sutherland	New Zealand	571 m (1,904 ft)
Mardalsfossen	Norway	509 m (1,696 ft)

MAJOR ISLANDS OF THE WORLD

Name	Sovereignty	Location	Area ('000)
Greenland	Denmark	N. Atlantic	2,176 sq km (840 sq mi)
New Guinea	Papua New Guinea and Indonesia	S.W. Pacific	793 sq km (306 sq mi)
Borneo	Indonesia, Malaysia and Brunei	S.W. Pacific	725 sq km (280 sq mi)
Madagascar	Madagascar	W. Indian Ocean	588 sq km (227 sq mi)
Baffin	Canada	Canadian Arctic	477 sq km (184 sq mi)
Sumatra	Indonesia	E. Indian Ocean	474 sq km (183 sq mi)
Honshu	Japan	N.W. Pacific	231 sq km (89 sq mi)
Great Britain	United Kingdom	N.E. Atlantic	218 sq km (84 sq mi)

MAJOR DESERTS OF THE WORLD

Name	Location	Area ('000)
Sahara	North America	7,770 sq km (3,000 sq mi)
Australian	Australia	1,684 sq km (650 sq mi)
Arabian	S.W. Asia	1,295 sq km (500 sq mi)
Gobi	Mongolia/China	1,295 sq km (500 sq mi)

MAJOR LAKES OF THE WORLD

Name	Location	Area ('000)
Caspian Sea	Asia	373 sq km (144 sq mi)
Superior	Canada/U.S.A.	83 sq km (32 sq mi)
Victoria	Kenya/Tanzania/Uganda	70 sq km (27 sq mi)
Aral Sea	Kazakstan-Uzbekistan	65 sq km (25 sq mi)
Huron	Canada/U.S.A.	60 sq km (23 sq mi)
Michigan	U.S.A.	57 sq km (22 sq mi)
Tanganyika	Zaire/Zambia/Tanzania/Burundi	34 sq km (13 sq mi)
Great Bear	Canada	31 sq km (12 sq mi)
Baykal	Russia	31 sq km (12 sq mi)

PRINCIPAL MOUNTAIN PEAKS OF THE WORLD

Name	Location	Height
Everest	Nepal/Tibet	8,708 m (29,028 ft)
Godwin-Austen	Pakistan-China	8,475 m (28,250 ft)
Kanchenjunga	India/Nepal	8,462 m (28,208 ft)
Nanga Parbat	Kashmir	7,998 m (26,660 ft)
Gasherbrum	Kashmir	7,941 m (26,470 ft)
Aconcagua	Argentina	6,859 m (22,201 ft)
Illimani	Bolivia	6,360 m (21,201 ft)
McKinley	Alaska, U.S.A.	6,096 m (20,320 ft)
Logan	Canada	5,955 m (19,850 ft)
Cotopaxi	Ecuador	5,865 m (19,550 ft)
Kilimanjaro	Tanzania	5,802 m (19,340 ft)
Citlaltepec	Mexico	5,610 m (18,700 ft)
Damavand	Iran	5,582 m (18,606 ft)
Ararat	Turkey	5,084 m (16,945 ft)

PRINCIPAL RIVERS OF THE WORLD

Name	Location	Length
Nile	Africa	6,673 km (4,145 mi)
Amazon	South America	6,440 km (4,000 mi)
Mississippi-Missouri	U.S.A.	5,973 km (3,710 mi)
Ob'Irtysh	Russia-Kazakstan	5,571 km (3,460 mi)
Yangtse-Kiang	China	5,474 km (3,400 mi)
Hwang-Ho	China	4,830 km (3,000 mi)
Congo	Africa	4,376 km (2,718 mi)
Amur	Asia	4,347 km (2,700 mi)
Lena	Russia	4,315 km (2,680 mi)
Mackenzie-Peace	Canada	4,242 km (2,635 mi)
Mekong	Asia	4,186 km (2,600 mi)
Niger	West Africa	4,186 km (2,600 mi)
Yenisey	Russia	4,131 km (2,566 mi)
Parana	South America	4,025 km (2,500 mi)
Murray-Darling	Australia	3,719 km (2,310 mi)
Volga	Russia	3,687 km (2,290 mi)
Euphrates	Asia	3,598 km (2,235 mi)
Danube	Europe	2,859 km (1,776 mi)
Zambezi	Africa	2,737 km (1,700 mi)

SECTION FOUR

HISTORY

PREHISTORY – A.D. 400

Man in Prehistory

The species to which modern man belongs is identifiable from fossils and remains of some 40,000 – 50,000 years ago. It is uncertain whether older remains that have been found form part of the direct ancestry of man, or are extinct offshoots of the mainstream. During the late Old Stone Age (from *c.* 30,000 B.C.), man invented tools to serve the various activities of hunting, fishing, carving, and began to evolve individual, local cultures.

Development took different forms and occurred at different rates, depending on geographic and climatic conditions. During the last Ice Age (*c.* 30,000 – 8,000 B.C.), vegetable food and game were probably plentiful in the broad, tundra-like region at the edge of the ice-fields. When the ice receded in Europe, forests slowly appeared again and the hunting of animals became more difficult. The people settled on the shores of lakes, on river banks and in forests. Under the varied conditions, separate, yet in many instances parallel, growth and development followed.

Mesopotamia

In the warmer climates the process of civilization was more rapid, particularly in such fertile river valleys as the Danube, the Nile, the Euphrates and the Tigris.

Babylonia and the eastern mediterranean kingdoms, about 1400 B.C.

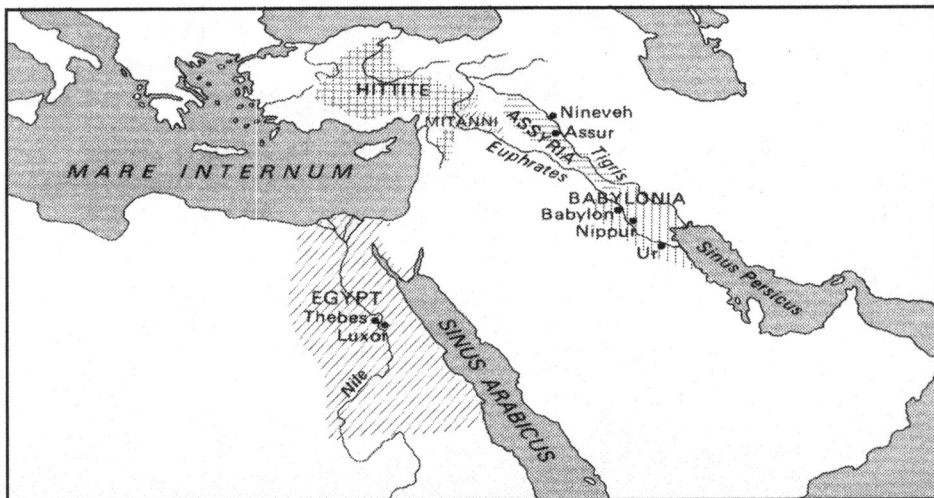

By 6000 B.C., the major steps of grain cultivation and animal domestication had been taken. During the next 1,500 years, the working of metals was discovered and copper came into common use. The communities then lived by farming and hunting.

Communities grew into towns, occupations became specialized and community leaders emerged with religious and political functions. Migratory groups settled down, land was cultivated annually, manured and irrigated. By 3000 B.C. the art of writing and scientific pursuits were well established. Bronze had been developed; in Mesopotamia, the height of Bronze Age culture was reached between 3000 and 2000 B.C.

As the populations grew, waves of migratory groups made for the fertile valleys. Sumerians, Akkadians, Babylonians, Hittites and Assyrians gained, lost and regained sway over the principal cities of Mesopotamia — Ur, Nippur, Babylon, Nineveh, Assur and others.

Egypt and the Mediterranean

The civilizations of Egypt formed a separate, parallel centre of human development. Except for brief periods, it remained independent of Mesopotamian culture until the 7th century B.C. when Ashurbanipal (669–626 B.C.), an Assyrian king, conquered Egypt. The Assyrian empire was, in turn, destroyed by the Medes, Persians and Chaldeans. Under Cyprus (c. 600–529 B.C.), the Persian Empire stretched from the Mediterranean far into India.

For about 600 years, from 2000 B.C. to 1400 B.C., a cultured, artistic and scientific civilization flourished in Crete. After that Crete, along with the Aegean islands and the mainland of Greece, was overrun by invaders from Macedonia, north of Greece. From the middle centuries of the 1st millenium B.C., the Phoenicians became renowned as traders over the entire length of the Mediterranean and possibly beyond — as far as Scilly Isles and Senegal.

China and India

The civilization of China had also reached an advanced state by 1000 B.C.. Although it probably developed independently of the cultures in western Asia, it progressed along similar lines — villages developing into city states, settlements located around rivers, the invention of writing.

Indian civilization, which is at least as old as those of western Asia, had also achieved a high level of mercantile and political organization and domestic comfort. About 1500 B.C., the Aryan people began to conquer northern India, and eventually spread across the entire subcontinent, settling in small agricultural communities. It was during this early period of Indian history that the Vedic text and the hymns of the Rigveda were first set down.

A.D. 400–1350

Roman Empire

By A.D. 400, the Roman Empire, the principal cohesive force in the West during the first three centuries after Jesus Christ, was on the wane. The emperor had removed to Constantinople, a move which eventually split the empire. It resulted in the rise of the bishopric of Rome as the prime power of Christianity and a political force in its own right. Ascetic reaction to the wealth and worldliness of the Church led, through such men as Jerome (*c.* 340–420), Ambrose 7–(*c.* 340–397) and Augustine (354–430), to the foundation of monasticism.

The declining strength of the Roman Empire allowed first the Huns and Goths, then the Franks and Vandals, to invade the provinces and eventually to sack Rome, which was reduced from its imperial glory to the status of a decrepit provincial town. In 800, Charlemagne (742–814), a Frankish king, was crowned emperor. However, his empire, extending over the whole of Europe except for Britain and Scandinavia, was basically Germanic in character and traditions. The coronation of Charlemagne also caused the definitive break between Rome and the Byzantine half of the empire, ruled from Constantinople, since the eastern Roman emperor regarded Charlemagne as a usurper. After Charlemagne's death, the cohesion of the empire was lost again, this time, forever. Muslims invaded Spain, Scandinavians raided the north, and the empire was divided among Charlemagne's family.

The Byzantine Empire, however, remained intact, extending over the whole of the eastern Mediterranean and into Mesopotamia. Rich, aristocratic, religious, colourful and artistic, it reached its height in the 10th and 11th centuries.

Charlemagne being crowned Holy Roman Emperor by Pope Leo III

136

Islam

During this period, the Muslim faith was founded in Mecca by Mohammed (570–632). To the east, Islam spread to Syria and Persia; to the west, along the southern coast of the Mediterranean and, in 711, into Spain.

Great Islamic centres of learning developed. Astronomy, mathematics and alchemy were extensively studied. In the 9th century, a House of Knowledge was instituted in Baghdad. This House of Knowledge became immensely important through its translation and preservation of the works of Hippocrates (c. 460–377 B.C.), Euclid (c. 450–374 B.C.), Aristotle (384–322 B.C.), Galen (2nd cent. A.D.) and Ptolemy (2nd cent. A.D.). Without this store of knowledge and its transmission into modern European culture through Spain, much of the Greek scientific work would have been lost.

The Crusades

In the late 11th century, the Christian states of Europe began their attempts to reconquer the lands under Muslim domination. Backed by various popes, the movement was blessed with the status of a Holy War. Over a period of 200 years, a number of Crusades set out to conquer the eastern Mediterranean lands and capture Jerusalem.

The Crusades often caused as much disruption in Europe as they did in the Middle East. Polyglot bands, internecine arguments and ineffectual leadership were common, to the detriment of the European countryside through which the Crusaders marched.

Throughout this period, the feudal aristocracy of Europe was becoming more powerful and less inclined to bow before monarchs. In 1215, King John of England (c. 1167–1216) was forced to sign the Magna Carta, which subjected the English monarchy to one of the earliest forms of constitutional control in the world.

The Mongols

As the Crusaders trudged eastwards, the Mongols were galloping out of Asia towards Europe. Under Batu Khan (d. 1255), they reached Hungary. Previously, with Genghis Khan (c. 1162–1227) at their head, the Mongols had established hegemony throughout Asia, failing only to invade Japan.

The threat of the Mongols encouraged a great sense of unity amongst the Japanese clans and tribes, which had been divided into shifting, warring factions for centuries. A long period of imitation of Chinese culture, particularly its literature and paintings, slowly gave way to indigenous forms. This created a revival of the Shinto religion and a strong period of Zen Buddhism.

South America

Across the Pacific Ocean, cut off from the rest of the world, there developed the main South American civilizations of the Aztecs, the Mayas and the Incas. Although the principle of the wheel and the manufacture of iron were unknown to them, their civilizations had developed to a high degree, particularly in the fields of astronomy, mathematics and architecture. Complex and elaborate cities were inhabited by their highly developed hierarchic society, with peasants, soldiers, administrators and priests being subservient to an emperor who claimed divine birth. Eventually, they were invaded and destroyed by the Spanish conquistadors.

1350–1600

European Society

This period saw fundamental changes in the structure of European society. The mercantile class grew in strength, and political power rested in land and wealth rather than heredity. In 1337, the Hundred Years' War broke out between England and France, precipitated by commercial rivalry.

The Holy Roman Empire ceased to be a monarchy and became instead a collection of federated, individual states. The Moors were driven from Spain and a gradual unification of the Spanish principalities and kingdoms followed. Ivan III (1440–1505) founded the modern Russian state through conquest of territory and by his marriage to a Byzantine princess, thus making the Russians custodians of the Eastern Orthodox religion.

The decline of the Byzantine Empire symbolized in this union accompanied the rise of the Ottoman Turks, who, by 1529, had conquered south-eastern Europe as far as the walls of Vienna. They fought constantly with the Venetians who were also engaged in a struggle for power involving the city states and kingdoms of Italy.

The Reformation

Anarchy reigned in Rome. Pope Clement V, a Frenchman, never set foot in Italy, and from 1309 to 1375, the popes held court at Avignon. During this time, the rights, privileges and finances of the papacy were reorganized. The papal claim to absolute jurisdiction over clergy of any nationality, abuses of wealth and privilege, and internal schisms (which caused two popes to be elected in 1378) promoted adverse reaction throughout Europe.

Such men as John Hus (1369–1415), a Bohemian, and John Wiclif (c. 1320–84), an Englishman, initiated the cause of a vernacular religion free from abuses. The Reformation was openly demanded in 1517 by Martin Luther (1483–1546). The critical scholarship of Desiderius Erasmus (c. 1466–1536) did much to foster it. Luther's appeal was echoed by Huldreich Zwingli (1484–1531) and John Calvin (1509–64) in Switzerland, by John Knox (1505–72) in Scotland and others throughout Europe.

In 1534, Henry VIII (1491–1547) was declared Supreme Head of the Church and Clergy of England. Although done for personal motives, it marked a break from Rome which was reinforced under Elizabeth I (1533–1603) in 1563.

In France, protestantism, observed by the Huguenots who formed a large minority, caused a series of intense civil wars. Spain never accepted protestantism. To counter it, St. Ignatius Loyola (1491–1556) founded the Society of Jesus in 1534.

Humanism and the Renaissance

The influence of Erasmus was indicative of the wide spread of the humanistic philosophy which developed out of Italy. Rooted in the philosophy of Plato (*c.* 427–347 B.C.), it was expressed not only in religious and philosophical works, but in the immensely rich media of painting, sculpture and architecture which developed in Italy and spread throughout Europe. A new respect for the individuality of each human being and the renewed appeal of the classical ideals of harmony and balance gave rise to the artistic and scientific achievements of Leonardo da Vinci (1452–1519), Michelangelo (1475–1564) and Raphael (1483–1520).

The sciences developed concurrently, particularly in the fields of anatomy — man's examination of himself — and astronomy — his attempt to comprehend the boundaries of the physical universe.

Raphael's painting of 'The Disputation Concerning the Blessed Sacrament'

The momentum of the Renaissance was accelerated by the invention of the printing press in Europe (although similar processes had been used much earlier in China) which enabled the new thoughts and discoveries to be disseminated much more rapidly. Through it, the Bible, translated into the languages of the common people of Europe, reached a far wider and more critical audience than ever before.

Missions and Discoveries

The biblical word was carried out of Europe. Many discoverers, such as Henry the Navigator (1394–1460), were prompted in their travels largely by religious motives. Henry explored the coast of Africa; Vasco da Gama (c. 1469–1524) journeyed to India; Christoper Columbus (1451–1506) sailed across the Atlantic, searching for the Indies; Vasco Nunez de Balboa (1475–1519) sighted the Pacific and Ferdinand Magellan (c. 1480–1521) sailed into it.

For such journeys, shipbuilding advanced, better navigational instruments were manufactured, and charts drawn up. In Europe, rapid deforestation led to a great expansion in the coal-mining industry. More powerful furnaces led to advances in metallurgy. New crops were introduced from the lands visited by the explorers, and new machines were developed to cultivate those already known.

The new technology of printing enabled the publication of many works on the developing scientific and industrial scene. The process was rapidly advanced by Johann Gutenberg (c. 1400–68), who developed movable metal type, thereby greatly increasing the speed of typesetting books. Moreover, with greater accuracy and flexibility in the process of making wood-blocks, the books were enhanced by illustrations. Among the important books printed at the time were *De Re Aedificatoria,* by Leon Battista Alberti (1404–72), which discussed the art and technology of architecture, and *Pyrotechnica*, by Vannocio Boringuccio (1480–

1539), which was the first practical textbook on all aspects of metallurgy. *De Re Metallica,* by Georgius Agricola (1494–1555), was a comprehensive handbook on the mining industry and dealt not only with the technical aspects, but also the health and social welfare of the miners. It was one of the earliest examples of concern for the social implications of the shift from farming to industrial society.

1600–1800

Four revolutions, vital to the present state of the world, occurred during this period. Three were political; one, the most fundamental, was industrial.

The Industrial Revolution
First introduced in the English textile industry, the process of mechanization transformed the lives of the men and women involved. The principal place of work shifted from cottage to factory. As the factories needed more workers, towns grew to house them, and a prolonged movement of people away from the countryside and agriculture began. Steam power and engineering advanced, and iron production increased, rapidly. Transport, by road and canal, and communications were systematically improved. The process of industrialization spread all over Western Europe. Important pottery centres, such as those at Delft and Sèvres, were formed, making use of improved furnaces to fire their ware.

For those who had to produce the goods, conditions in the expanding, often unplanned, towns frequently promoted disease, distress and antagonism towards the owners of the factories who were rapidly growing richer.

An early steam carriage used in England

The storming of the Bastille at the start of the French Revolution

The Political Revolutions

In England, America, and France, economic, religious and intellectual reasons combined to overthrow the ruling governments. The English Civil War began in 1642. On one side were parliamentary power, merchant wealth, puritanism and belief in the sovereignty of the individual conscience over institutional authority; on the other, the 'Divine Right' of kings and bishops to rule, and the attempts by Charles I (1600–49) to rule and raise money without the authority of Parliament. The parliamentarians won and the King was executed. However, after the death of Cromwell (1599–1658), the monarchy was restored under Parliament's authority.

By the 18th century, Britain's American colonies had established an identity of their own. British repression of moves towards more self-governance served to unite the colonies. The revolutionary war of 1775–83 bound them together still further, ensuring that independence would be granted to the United States.

The American success was an important spur to the revolutionaries in France. There, the widening gap between the extravagant taste of the king and his court, and the oppressed people whose taxes provided the revenue, led them to demand a new constitution. Under it, many feudal titles and privileges were abolished. The impetus generated, however, was too strong for moderate reform. The revolution became more extreme and turned bloody: hundreds followed Louis XVI (1754–93) to the guillotine.

Philosophy

A visible link existed between the American and French revolutions: the works of Thomas Paine (1737–1809). In 1776, his pamphlet *Common Sense* greatly influenced American public opinion in favour of independence; in 1791, he published *The Rights of Man* in defence of the aims of the French Revolution. Paine was among a number of philosophers in the second half of the 18th century who considered, as a whole, the situation of man in society. Jeremy Bentham (1748–1832) dealt with morals and welfare and Adam Smith (1723–90) the economic structure of society. They worked at a time when such men as John Locke (1632–1704), Pierre Bayle (1647–1706), George Berkeley (1685–1753), Voltaire (1694–1778) and David Hume (1711–76) were delving into man's capacity for knowledge and reason and their application in his daily life. This intensive, critical examination of man was carried into other fields.

Art and Science

Artists, mathematicians, sculptors, physicists and chemists enquired into the conventions and assumptions that they had inherited. In astronomy, concepts of the universe changed dramatically, throwing into doubt the theologically orientated notions of the mediaeval European world. Heat, magnetism and electricity began to be understood and, largely through the work of Sir Isaac Newton (1642–1727), the nature of light and laws of motion were first explained. Many of the organs of the human body were accurately described for the first time.

Colonization

Such searching energy also found an outlet in territorial expansion through colonization. Spain and Portugal acquired vast areas of South America, destroying such ancient civilizations as the Inca in the process. The Portuguese, Dutch, British and Prussians began to occupy parts of Africa. Trade wars between the European nations were common; during this time the British and French competed for commerce and territory in India.

Such incursions in India were made possible by the gradual dismemberment of the Mogul Empire, which broke up after the death of its last great leader, Aurangzib (1618–1707). The Mongols were eventually driven out of China, whose population was growing rapidly, and who made its own territorial acquisition by invading Tibet. Farther east, Japan entered a period of strict isolation and political conservatism under the Tokugawa shogunate. Economic decline, internal debt, famine and natural disasters gave rise to fierce riots and social upheaval in 1787.

1800–1970s

Technology

In Europe and America, the period was one of ever-accelerating change in technology. In 1865, an Act of Parliament in Britain restricted the speed of all road vehicles to 6 kilometres per hour (3.7 m.p.h.) or less. Within a hundred years, men were orbiting the earth at thousands of kilometres an hour, intent on travelling to the moon. Comparable rates of change occurred in many other areas of technology, made possible largely by the increased sophistication of machine tools, which enabled more and more complex engineering and manufacturing processes to be carried out rapidly and repeatedly.

The advantages technology brought, throughout the 19th century at least, did little for the well-being of the masses. The population increased more rapidly every year. With it, the feelings of anger and frustration at the unequal distribution of wealth and power, which had triggered the English Civil War and the French Revolution, manifested themselves frequently. Revolutions occurred throughout Europe, striving to achieve either a more liberal form of monarchy, a more representative government, or the abolition of monarchical and aristocratic rule.

Colonialism

On the basis of their industrial wealth, the powerful European nations attempted to create and consolidate world-wide colonial empires. During the reign of Queen Victoria (1819–1901), British troops were almost permanently engaged somewhere in the world extending or maintaining British influence over the countries which supplied raw materials to British factories. The Germans, French, British, Dutch and Portuguese contended for colonies in Africa and the Far East. The Russians sought naval access to the Mediterranean and pressed southwards against the British in Afghanistan.

The United States of America

One principal area of the world was closed to colonization. In 1823, James Monroe (1758–1831), President of the United States, proclaimed the 'Monroe Doctrine', forbidding further colonization by European powers of the American continents. During the century, the United States grew in size from the original eastern seaboard states to reach the Pacific Ocean. The Indians were overcome, the northern and southern frontiers defined. The Union itself was given its most severe test in the Civil War of 1861–65. Under the leadership of Abraham Lincoln (1809–65), the United States was strengthened in the form it has retained ever since.

144

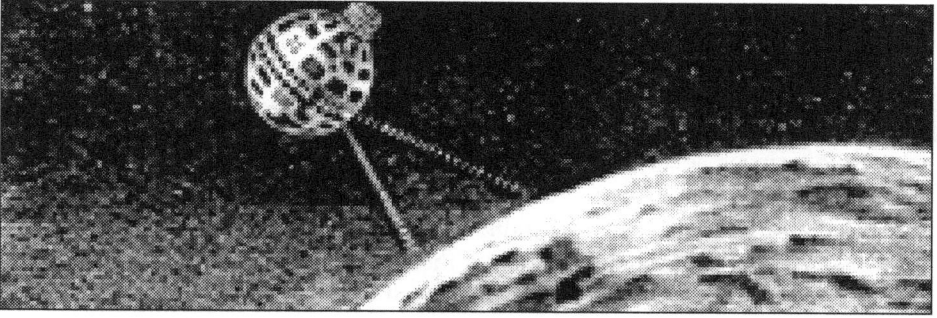

Telstar I came into use on 10 July 1962 — the first time live television pictures were relayed across the Atlantic.

China

In the Far East, European colonial interests in China vied with the territorial acquisitions of Japan, which continued until the end of the Second World War. Since the revolution in 1911, which overthrew the Manchu dynasty, China has been governed as a republic, first by Nationalists and then, since 1949, by the Communist government created by Mao Tse-tung (1893–1976).

Nationalism and Communism

The conflict between Nationalists and Communists was, and still is, a recurrent one in many parts of the world. It was the exaggerated polarization of such political forces which brought Hitler (1889–1945) to power in Germany at the head of a National Socialist regime. Victory for the Communists over the reactionary government of the Russian royal family brought about the foundation of the U.S.S.R. in 1917, an event which exacerbated international tensions and led, after 1945, to the division of the world into two power blocs.

Internationalism

Out of the nationalistic rivalries of the First and Second World Wars, a solution to international conflict was seen to lie in an organization to which all disputes should be referred. The League of Nations, set up after the First World War, failed to achieve its purpose. The United Nations has been more successful, but international power still resides with the richest and most heavily-armed nations.

Progress

The progression from horse and canal transport to rocket engines and spacecraft has not altered the nature of international politics, only the machinery. Electronic communications, although encircling the world, do not feed the majority of the world's population who have less than enough to eat.

1980 – 2000

Technology
The growth of technology which began in the previous century culminated in man conquering space, to the extent that today, private citizens who can afford it, can journey into space. The increased location of orbiting satellites has improved the use of all forms of communication. The cellular phone has grown in use and importance; matched only by the rise of the computer which has heralded in the arrival of E-commerce and the globalization of world trade.

Politics
This period witnessed the demise of apartheid in South Africa. The crumbling of the Berlin Wall, leading to a reunified Germany, culminated in the dismantling of the USSR and the break up of the Balkan States. This closed the chapter of the Cold War and the confrontational policies of nuclear arms. The break up of the Soviet Union and its satellites, however, created ethnic conflicts as it left only communist countries. This was replaced however by the rise of terrorism (and the possible looming of a religious war) with the Israeli-Arab conflicts posing a great threat to the stability of the world's new found peace.

Trade/Commerce
The emergence of China into the free world, followed the formation of the European Union of Nations, and the arrival of the WTO and its new rules for international trade, not the least of which was the increasing recognition of Intellectual Property Rights.

Threats to Human Existence
Technological developments led to concerns regarding the environment and the ability of the earth to sustain its increasing population and withstand the effects of global warming.

In addition, the increasing rise in the illegal use of drugs began to shake the pillars of society. At the same time, the scourge of HIV/AIDS decimated large portions of the African continent, and increasingly spread its threat across the world.

SECTION FIVE
ECONOMIC TERMS

Balance of payments.   A nation's accounts that shows payments by residents to and receipts from foreigners, resulting from international transactions. In other words, it is a nation's factual accounting of the relationship between the payments due to it (payment-claims or credits) and what it owes (payment-obligations or debits). Balance of payments covers 'visible exports', which are the receipts from sales to other countries of commodities produced in, or re-exported from, a nation. 'Visible imports' are the payments for goods imported. The 'invisibles' are the receipts from and payments for shipping, insurance and banking services, interests, profits and dividends, tourism, migrants' funds, gifts and legacies. All these form the current account of the balance of payments. The capital account shows the balance of lending between a nation and the rest of the world. The term balance of payments surplus or deficit is often applied to the current account section of the balance of payments.

Balance of trade.   Part of the current account section of the balance of payments, measured by the difference between a country's receipts for visible exports and its payments for visible imports.

When exports exceed imports, the difference is described as a balance of trade surplus, or 'active' balance; when imports exceed exports, the difference is a deficit, or 'passive' balance.

Bilateral trade.   SEE MULTILATERAL TRADE.

Boom.   A peak in the cycle of economic activity, when the economy is employed at full capacity. It also means an expansion of business activity.

Budget.   A formal estimate of income and expenditure over a period. In business and government it usually includes an indication of the policy to be pursued to achieve stated objectives.

A budget is a document which consists of both control and plan. It is "...a comprehensive advance plan of governmental revenues and expenditures and the taxes and other revenues required to finance them".

Capital.   The stock of resources available at a particular date to help satisfy future wants.

Copyright. Body of Legal rights that protect the work of authors and artists from being reproduced, performed or disseminated without permission.

Cost. That which is sacrificed in order to obtain anything. It implies the destruction or surrender of value on the performance of an activity. It may be measured in money or economic goods — money cost or real cost.
The approach to the measuring of cost generally accepted today is in terms of opportunities or alternatives forgone. This approach regards the cost of acquiring a good as the need to forgo the enjoyment of other goods if resources are used to produce it; therefore the cost of the good is the value of the alternatives forgone.

Cost of living. The monetary cost of maintaining a given standard or level of living.

Currency. The official medium of exchange or money of a country. A payment from one country to another is made in terms of the rate of exchange between the currencies involved.

Currency reform (monetary reform). In economics, currency or monetary reform is generally used to refer not so much to any legislative or administrative change in the monetary and banking system as to governmental action to reduce the claims against the economy which individuals and business firms hold in the form of money and time and savings deposits. Currency reform is also regarded as a step towards preventing inflation which impends.

Debt. A sum total of money, goods or services owed by a person or body to another. Modern economic society rests largely on debt — short-term and long-term. Some debts are created by the use of credit.

Deficiency payment. An amount, usually expressed in money terms, by which one sum is smaller than another to which it is related. It is usually measured as an excess of liabilities over assets. For example, a balance of payments deficit is an excess of imports of goods and services and financial claims over similar exports; a budget deficit is an excess of government expenditure over revenue in a financial year.

Deficit financing. Large-scale borrowing to meet a situation requiring large expenditure. It is a policy employed by government to alleviate unemployment or otherwise to stimulate the economy. Such financing usually increases the national debt.

Depreciation. Continued decrease in quantity, quality or value of an asset because of passage of time, wear and tear, obsolescence, fall in the market price or other causes.

148

In its most specific sense, depreciation refers to the diminished value and shortened life of capital goods that result from wear and tear. This decline in total usefulness is called depreciation.

Devaluation.   Reducing the value of the home currency in terms of foreign currencies. Devaluation denotes an act of government explicitly aimed at reducing the international value of its monetary unit in terms of those of other countries.

Embargo.   Originally, an order forbidding ships of a foreign power to enter or leave a country's ports. It has come to mean any suspension of a branch of commerce, e.g. an embargo on lending or the export of strategic commodities to unfriendly countries.

Exchange rates.   Prices quoted in one financial centre for the monetary balances available in another; the monetary unit of a country is given in terms of those of other countries.

Free economy.   One in which the main economic operations and processes are conducted by a private enterprise free of direct government control and activity.

Free enterprise.   A system in which the non-human factors of production are owned privately and are used to earn profits for their owners by producing goods and services. The system is free from excessive state regulation and direction but subject to laws on property, contract sale of goods, companies, restraints of trade, patents, copyrights and so on.

Free trade.   Trade unencumbered by tariffs, quotas or other devices obstructing the movement of goods between countries.

Free trade area.   An arrangement between two or more countries to eliminate customs and other trade barriers between themselves while allowing each to retain its tariffs against other countries.

Gross Domestic Product.   The money value of all goods and services produced in a nation during a stated period of time, normally a year.

Gross National Product.   The Gross Domestic Product of a country *plus* net income from abroad.

Hard currency.   One with a relatively stable value in international exchange. A currency is normally 'hard' because of the country's strong trading position, usually shown by a large and consistent surplus in the balance of current payments and internal stability.

Imports. Goods and services brought into a country by commerce. The difference between the imports and exports of a country as recorded by its customs department is called the balance of trade. The records made at the customs house refer to material commodities, but a country may be importing services (service imports) the value of which cannot be entered in the trade returns. They are usually called 'invisible' imports.

Incentive. A word encountered more frequently in economics than in any of the other social sciences. It tends to be used as a synonym for motivation to do work and is used particularly to denote the motivation of entrepreneurs and workers. In both cases, historically, the incentive was assumed to be material award; in one case profit and in the other wages.

Income Tax. A tax levied upon the incomes of individuals and corporate bodies. Income tax is imposed on a yearly basis at progressive rates.

Inflation. A condition of rising prices caused by excessive demand or increasing cost of production. It results in a decline in the purchasing power of the monetary unit.

Intellectual Property. This refers to the intangible work created by a particular person. Although immaterial, it has many commonalities with real property. For example, it is an asset which may be bought, sold, exchanged or given away at will. The four main categories of intellectual property include *patents, trademarks, copyrights* and *trade secrets*.

Intellectual Property Rights. Refers to the body of rights governing the reproduction of licensing, exchange, sale and protection of intellectual property.

Interest. The price paid for loanable funds. It is usually expressed as X per cent per year.

Investment. Exchanging one asset for another which is expected to produce a greater return over a period of time. In economics, investment is restricted to assets which can be valued in terms of money. In fact, most investments are in the form of money, although it must be seen as a means of exchange for other assets.

Invisible exports. So called because, like exports, they give rise to payments from people in other countries to residents, but without movements of goods between their countries. These payments are generally for shipping, banking, interest on loans, dividends, insurance, legacies, gifts and tourism. They can be regarded as the 'export' of services.

Labour. In its broadest sense is a basic factor of production used in combination with capital and land to produce commodities or render services; more specifically, it is the number of people working or available for work, or the amount of work done.

Licensing. A method of controlling or recording the number of suppliers of a product or service, the amount produced or sold, etc. Its economic effect depends on how restrictive it is. If it is confined to recording, i.e. for the purpose of taxation, it has little effect on supply and price. If it is designed to keep down the number of licences, as with cars or buildings, its effect is to raise the value of the goods or properties that are licensed by making them scarcer than they would otherwise be.

Liquidity. Generally the ease with which an asset can be turned into money. Assets range from cash, which is perfectly liquid, through short-term claims and longer term securities to durable consumption and producer goods (and works of art).

Market. In its general economic sense, a group of buyers and sellers who are in sufficiently close contact for the transactions between any pair of them to affect the terms on which the others buy and sell. Ultimately, every transaction in any commodity or service affects and is affected by every other.
A market is typically an institution that brings all sellers and buyers into communication with one another for the purpose of exchanging economic goods and money for current or future delivery. The interaction of sellers and buyers determines the unit prices and the quantities transacted. Thus, the market is an essential component of the price system and its effective functioning determines in considerable part the smooth functioning of the latter.
It is noteworthy that the term 'market' is by no means limited to a particular place. The overriding requirement is communication among sellers and buyers.

Mercantilism. The term denotes the principles of the mercantile system, sometimes understood as the identification of wealth with money; but more generally, the belief that the economic welfare of the state can only be secured by government regulation of a nationalistic character.

Mixed economy. One in which some means of production are privately owned while others are publicly owned; in which the allocation of resources and level of economic activity are decided partly by private individuals and firms and partly by the government and public corporations. Economic activity is determined by free-market transactions, modified by taxes and subsidies, credit and other controls.

Monetary policy.   Control of the banking and monetary system by the government to achieve stability of the currency, a favourable balance of payments, full employment or other objectives. The immediate objective is control over the supply of money and credit, or 'the state of liquidity of the whole economy'. It is aimed, therefore, at the financial institutions of a country, which may be regarded as forming a single large credit market.

Monetary policy may be applied through:

a)   interest rates;

b)   control of international capital movements;

c)   control over the terms of hire purchase credit;

d)   selective control over the lending activities of banks and other financial institutions, capital issues and so on.

Monetary reform.   See CURRENCY REFORM.

Money.   Any commodity widely accepted as a means of exchange and a measure of value in payment for goods and services, or in discharge of debts. Money may take the form of notes and coins of token or intrinsic value; but in the modern economy the total supply of money available exceeds the quantity of notes, etc. in circulation because of credit. Credit is also universally acceptable as a means of exchange and in settlement of debts (it is money too).

Money market.   In general terms, a financial centre where foreign and inland bills of exchange, foreign currency, bullion and so on are bought and sold.

Monopoly.   Control of the market by a single seller of a commodity or service (monopsony, in the case of a buyer).

Multilateral trade.   Trade among many countries. It is a means of extracting maximum gains from international trade and division of labour. The contrast is bilateral trade, in which one country makes an agreement to trade with another. Bilateralism limits consumers' freedom to buy goods from the cheapest market and prevents the realization of full international specialization with each country producing for export the products in which it has the largest comparative advantage.

Where trade is mutilateral, there is no need for a company to balance its payments to and from individual trading partners. It needs only to maintain balance of payments equilibrium between itself and the rest of the world as a whole.

If a country adopts bilateralism when the rest of the world is trading multilaterally and there are no serious problems of unemployment at home, it deprives itself of the advantages of free trade and lowers the standard of living of its inhabitants.

National debt.   The debt of the government accumulated by borrowing, on which interest is paid. It is the sum total of all the financial obligations resulting from the borrowing of all the government units — national, regional and local. It does not include those financial obligations of the government which are not the result of borrowing, e.g. gold certificates, currency, contractual obligations for goods and services; nor does it include the private debts of persons and corporations.

National income.   The total value of all goods and services made available in any period for consumption or for adding to wealth. It may be calculated as the sum of incomes or expenditures, which must be equal to each other since all expenditures in a country must generate an equal amount of incomes.

The national income is the total of incomes of all residents, companies and government bodies derived from the production of goods and services. Some incomes are not matched by current economic activity, e.g. old-age pensions, national insurance benefits, family allowances, interest on the national debt. They are called 'transfer payments' or 'transfer incomes' because the purchasing power they give the recipients has been obtained at the expense of other income receivers who are taxed to provide them. Transfer payments are therefore excluded from the national income. All other incomes, such as wages, salaries, interests, profits, dividends, rents, undistributed profits of companies and public corporations, are included.

National income is also the money value of expenditures on all goods and services which generate incomes within the country.

Nationalization.   It embraces two distinct ideas, those of national ownership and national control. In addition, it has been made to cover management of private property in the national interest.

Strictly, nationalization might be said to entail both ownership and control by the state. However, the term has been used to cover diverse schemes, ranging from ownership by the state with direct control by its officials to ownership or partial ownership by the state and control by independent or quasi-independent bodies including workers' unions. It has also been used to describe measures taken by governments to control industries in the national interest, with ownership remaining in private hands.

Output (productivity).   Output comprises all the goods and services resulting from the economic activities of an individual, a firm, an industry or a country. Output is normally taken to be gross output; but in the course of production the firm or country will have used goods and services produced by other firms or countries. A more useful definition of output therefore relates to gross output less the goods or services used in production; this amount is called net output.

The resources expended (the input) and the results obtained (the output) are generally expressed in terms of quantities, but output may be measured either in quantities or value units.

Price. The amount of money given in exchange for a commodity or service; in other words, the value of a commodity or service in terms of money. In buying goods and some services, it is called 'price'; in hiring labour services 'wages', 'salary', 'fee'; in borrowing money or capital 'interest'; in hiring land or building 'rent'.
A price is a measure, in terms of money or some other widely accepted commodity, of the exchange value of a good or service.

Price system. The term is used to denote a form of economic organization in which the allocation of economic resources among various possible uses is detemined by price. Hence, it connotes a system of rationing in which the chief guides to choice and action are prices. In a general sense, any economic system in which market prices play some part in guiding the allocation of economic resources makes use of the price system.

Private enterprise. The economic activities of a community which are independent of government control and directed to satisfy private wants.

Private sector. That part of an economic system which is independent of government control. Broadly, the private sector coincides with the productive activities operated by private enterprise. They include a wide range of organizations — from the one-man firm to the giant corporation, all managed by private individuals who seek to maintain or increase profits by selling the goods and services the public demand.

Productivity. See OUTPUT.

Profit. In everyday language, a surplus of income over expenses. Profit was once regarded as the wages paid to the entrepreneur for his work, as interest on capital.

Profits are the income (positive or negative) that arises because the economy is dynamic, i.e. because there is change. Profits (positive or negative) can be defined as returns to the exercise of these functions, call *entrepreneurial functions.*

Public enterprise. The term is used to denote enterprises which are public, i.e. not entirely operated by private individuals or groups. It applies to enterprises under state direction at national level, and in its broadest sense also includes those controlled by regional and local bodies. It denotes public services which are economic enterprises, i.e. which may be expected to pay for themselves. Education, the armed forces and the judiciary are public services which do not pay for themselves and are not, therefore, economic enterprises.

Public finance. The study of the nature and effects of the government's use of fiscal instruments — taxes and spending, borrowing and lending, buying and selling.

Public finance covers the financial methods, principles and procedures employed by the government (whether federal, national, state or local). It, therefore, has a primary concern with the pattern and channels of public spending and tax collection. The term also denotes the sub-field of economics in which the financial operations of governments and the impact of such operations upon the level of consumption, investment, production, employment, etc. are studied.

Public sector. That part of a nation's economic activities that comes within the scope of the central government, including social insurance, nationalized industries and other public corporations.

Rates. Taxes on property levied by local authorities in order to finance local public services and amenities.

Rent. Rent is payment to any factor of production which is in limited supply. It is also any surplus amount earned by reason of superior quality or ability.

Reserves. Earnings earmarked by a company or country for specified or general purposes. A country's reserves consist of gold and foreign currencies used for international trade. If a country is earning less than it is buying, it then draws from its reserves to make up the deficit. Reserves act as a buffer stock in preventing undesirable temporary fluctuations in trade or foreign exchange rates.

Retailing. Selling goods for final consumption or use to private consumers, usually in shops or stores but also from markets, stalls and door-to-door trading.

Revenue. A producer of economic goods and services refers to revenue as being the return he receives from his output for the market. Adam Smith stated that wages, profit and rent are the three original forms of revenue, and that land and capital stock are the two original sources of all revenue.

In economic analysis, under the theory of pricing or value theory, the terms total revenue, average revenue and marginal revenue are used.

Total revenue refers to total receipts, or all revenue derived from the sale of the entire output.

Average revenue refers to the total receipts divided by the number of units of product sold; under conditions of pure or perfect competition it is the price per unit.

Marginal revenue is the additional revenue derived from producing one more unit of product.

Gross revenue consists of the entire gross receipts with no costs or expenses deducted.

Net revenue is the profit after costs and expenses have been deducted.

Operating revenue, in the accounting of railroads and public utilities, is the gross receipts from services.

Government revenue, or *public revenue*, includes all public monies which the state receives from whatever source, with the exception of loans, even though they add to current receipts. Government revenue includes taxes, fines, licence fees, special assessments, income from publicly owned enterprises and miscellaneous receipts, such as proceeds from the sale of publicly owned properties, interest on government funds, etc.

Saving.   The term saving denotes:
(*a*) the process of accumulating money or material goods for future use;
(*b*) the money or goods that are so accumulated;
(*c*) the process of conserving resources;
(*d*) the resources that are retained by such conservation.

In economics, saving in sense (*a*) is treated as the forgoing of consumption to accumulate assets. The outcome of such a process is saving in sense (*b*). In analytical terms, saving in sense (*b*) is the excess of income over expenditure on consumption.

Scarcity.   In economics, the lack of a commodity in relation to the demand for it. Most goods and services are scarce because, at any given time, the supplies of raw material, machinery, land and labour needed to create them are scarce. Economic scarcity is normally measured by value or by price in relation to the prices of other things.

Security.   Economists use the term to denote a financial pledge which is, at the same time, a form of investment.

Soft currency.   One with a relatively unstable value in international exchange or whose external value tends to fall in the long run. Normally, a currency is soft because of the weakness of the country's balance of payments, which may be in deficit for long periods.

Speculation.   In economics, it denotes the action of forecasting fluctuations in the prices of commodities or stocks, and buying and selling them in order to profit from the anticipated price changes.

Subsidy.   A government grant of money to industries to raise their incomes or lower the prices of their products, or encourage exports, etc.

Tariff.   Tariffs are custom duties which are used to yield revenue for the government or to protect home industries from the competition of imports.
There are three major ways in which a tariff may be imposed; *ad valorem tariff,* which is imposed as a percentage of the price of the imported product; *specific tariff,* which is imposed as a levy of so much per unit of an imported product; and *combined duty,* if a product is subject to one or the other duty, depending on which is lower.

Tax, Direct and Indirect.   A direct tax is levied directly on the taxpayer, e.g. income tax; surtax, estate duty, private car licence, local rates; an indirect tax is levied indirectly, e.g. excise duty on beer and spirits, purchase tax, custom duty on imported textiles, cameras, clocks, cars. This distinction is administrative rather than economic; thus the car tax is administratively direct but economically indirect since it must be paid if the customer is to use the car.

Taxation.   Charges on income, property, commodities and services to finance the conduct of government and services such as defence, public utilities, communications, education, health, housing, pensions, etc. They are paid by persons, partnerships or companies to the central government, when they are called taxes, or to local authorities, when they are called rates.
Taxation is levied by the government on those subject to its jurisdiction (individuals, groups, corporations) with little regard to benefits bestowed. Taxation is generally thought of as an instrument of revenue, but revenue is not the only purpose of taxation. It is also employed to regulate the production and consumption of certain goods and is regarded as a major instrument of national economic policy.

Terms of trade.   A measure of the purchasing power of exports in terms of imports. When import prices rise relatively to export prices, the terms of trade worsen; when export prices rise relatively to import prices the terms of trade improve. The usual measure of the terms of trade is an index calculated by dividing an index of export prices by an index of import prices. A rise in the index in one year compared with the previous year means a favourable movement in the terms of trade, and vice versa.

Trade cycle. Alternating periods of rising and falling levels of economic activity, with accompanying fluctuation in employment, wages, prices, profits and production. A typical cycle consists of a period of expansion, a downturn or recession, a period of contraction, and an upturn or revival.

Wages. In the broadest economic sense, the reward of the factor of production labour. Wages are the price of labour.

SECTION SIX
INFORMATION TECHNOLOGY

ABBREVIATIONS

ALU – Arithmetic Logic Unit
CAD – Computer Aided Design
CPU – Central Processing Unit
HTML – Hypertext Markup Language
MOUS – Microsoft Office User Specialist
PC – Personal Computer
RDS – Relational Database System
SQL – Structured Query Language
URL – Uniform Resource Locator
WWW – World Wide Web

COMPUTER TERMS

E-mail: Electronic messages sent to and from other users on a computer network.

Hypertext Markup Language: Used to create and establish links between web pages.

Icons: Small pictures used to represent programs, files, or functions in a meaningful way.

Internet: A massive collection of computer networks that connect millions of computers, people, software programs, databases and files worldwide.

Intranet: A private network within an organization which uses the same hardware and software as the Internet.

Network: Any two or more computers connected together to share resources or communicate.

Protocol: A communication standard. Computers must use the same protocols (languages) in order to communicate.

Search Engines: Search engines such as Lycos, Yahoo and Infoseek help to find information when browsing on the web.

Watermark: A lightly shaded image that appears to underly a document text.

Web Pages: Web pages are documents created to publish information on the Internet.

Web Server: A PC that stores web pages that may be accessed by other computers on an Intranet or on the Internet.

Word Wrap: Texture of a word processor that automatically places soft returns.

World Wide Web: The World Wide Web is the software, protocols, conventions and information that enable hypertext and multimedia publishing of resources on different computers around the world.

COMPUTER CRIMES

Trojan Horse: A program designed to breach a computer's security system while performing a seemingly harmless task.

Data Diddling: Purposely altering data as it is entered into the computer. Sometimes used to disguise illicit activities.

Worm: A program which has the ability to reproduce itself across a network, usually with a harmful effect.

COMPUTER PARTS AND THEIR USES

The mechanical and electronic devices used in a computer system are called *Computer Hardware.* The following are standard hardware components for computer systems:

Monitor (Output Device):   This enables the user to view what is currently being processed by the computer.

Central Processing Unit: Computers contain electronic processors which process data and control the operation of the computer system.

RAM and ROM: Housed in the same case as the processor is RAM (Random Access Memory) which acts as a temporary storage area for data being processed. Programs which are vital to starting up the computer are permanently stored in ROM (Read Only Memory).

Keyboard: This enables the user to type information into the computer.

Mouse: This small hand-held device causes a pointer to move across your screen as you move the mouse on your desktop. It has buttons which you can click in order to make selections or move things around on your screen.

Diskette Drive (floppy drive):   A mechanical recording device which reads from or writes information onto diskettes on which computer files may be permanently stored. Diskettes may be inserted and removed from your floppy drive.

Hard Disk Drive: A device which stores computer files. Hard drives are installed within the CPU and are not removed from the computer during normal operation.

Zip Drives: Zip drives are similar to diskette drives in that they are removable and at the same time similar to hard drives in that they store a large volume of data.

Printer: This enables the user to obtain printed output of work done on the computer. There are a few operations which may not require the use of a printer, hence having a printer is not always essential.

Multimedia Kit: These kits consist of (but are not limited to) speakers, microphone, video camera and CD-ROM drives. CD-ROM drives are used for permanent storage of applications and data on compact disks.

Computer hardware functions only as directed by computer programs. Programs contain instructions to the system as to what processes would be carried out by the computer. Computer programs are often referred to as *Software*. Various programming languages may be used to develop *Software Packages*. These have menu options and commands which have specific command formats or usage. When a computer program is purchased, a manual of instructions on its use is normally provided. Some examples of software packages developed for specific applications include:

Word Processors: Used for preparation of written matter, including correspondence, documents such as contracts, books and theses, to name a few.

Databases: Used for collecting and storing a large volume of information in a well organized format and processing the information by sorting in alphabetical, numeric or chronological order, performing enquiries to extracting required information.

Spreadsheets: Spreadsheets are documents set up in a format of columns and rows. They are used for a wide variety of purposes, often involving calculations and complex formulae.

Computer Games: Games (card games, pinball, pacman, etc.) of all sorts used for entertainment.

SECTION SEVEN
THE STUDENT'S DIRECTORY

UNIVERSITIES AND COLLEGES

The University of the West Indies serves the Caribbean territories with campuses at Cave Hill in Barbados, St. Augustine in Trinidad and Mona in Jamaica. Each campus will supply, on request, all necessary information on any course offered in the Arts, Science and Social Sciences, be it a degree, diploma or certificate course.

Applications to foreign universities and colleges are best made direct. Books listing universities and colleges throughout the Commonwealth and in America can be found in the public libraries.

The Embassy, High Commission or Consulate of any country will also supply, on request, information on all its universities and colleges.

QUALIFICATIONS

All universities and colleges have set minimum qualifications for entry. The University of the West Indies' minimum entry requirement is either four CXC General / 'O' Levels and three 'A' Levels or the CAPE equivalent or five CXC General / 'O' Levels and two 'A' Levels. There is also a faculty requirement, which is flexible in some cases. For example, if you wish to study for a degree in History, the normal History Faculty requirement is at least a CXC General / 'O' Level in History. This is apart from the university requirement, which must be met.

It is also important to have the right qualifications for entry to a university course. For example, if you wish to study Medicine, an 'A' Level in Religious Knowledge or Cookery will not get you into the Medicine Faculty. A teacher can be most helpful in advising you on the right qualifications for a course. The university or any students' advisory board will also help in providing information on the relevant qualifications for a course.

U.T.E.C.H.

The University of Technology (U.T.E.C.H.) in Kingston offers basically technical courses. It confers certificates, diplomas and degrees. Information on courses offered and qualifications required will be supplied by U.T.E.C.H. on application.

SCHOOL OF CONTINUING STUDIES

The School of Continuing Studies is affiliated to the University of the West Indies. It offers professional courses as well as Ordinary, Advance Levels and CXC study subjects. The department does not confer degrees or diplomas. For information on courses and subjects offered, write to the Director of Studies, School of Continuing Studies, 2 Camp Road, Kgn. 5.

SCHOLARSHIP

A scholarship is an award given on the basis of one's performance in an examination. The value of a scholarship usually covers the cost of a university course, except in Medicine where it covers only four-fifths of the cost. There are, however, different types of scholarships, so when applying for a scholarship, be sure you know what it covers.

The Ministry of Education administers a number of scholarships tenable at the University of the West Indies and elsewhere. Scholarships which are not administered by the Ministry include:

(*a*) The Rhodes Scholarship, which is tenable at Oxford University. It is awarded annually on the recommendation of the Committee of Selection to the Rhodes Trustees.

(*b*) Technical Assistance Study Fellowship, granted annually to post-graduates, under the terms and conditions of Development Projects, and financed by Overseas Aid.

Foreign embassies also offer scholarships for further studies in their countries. They will let you have all the necessary information on request. The University of the West Indies also has numerous scholarships and awards. It will give you the necessary information on application.

BURSARY

A bursary is an award based on academic achievement in examinations, departmental reports which show satisfactory academic progress and good conduct. Bursaries are awarded to registered students in educational institutions. They are not given as financial assistance, merely as awards of merit.

GRANTS

There are many types of grants but usually it covers the cost of boarding during a term, whether on or off campus. Grants do not cover the cost of tuition, books, clothing, equipment and materials. The rules, however, are flexible.

The Students' Loan Bureau offers grants and various loans. On request, you will be supplied with all the necessary information.

The University of the West Indies also offers various grants and loans. On application, it will let you know about its grants and loans.

ACADEMIC QUALIFICATIONS

THE DEGREE
The degree is the award of a university on the successful completion of study. There are three levels:

1. *The first degree is the Bachelors Degree.*

   This degree is awarded at the end of, normally, three academic years at a university, on successful completion of a course of study. The Bachelors Degree is classified into three categories;

   (*a*) 1st Class Honours;

   (*b*) 2nd Class Honours of Upper and Lower Division;

   (*c*) Pass.

   The exceptions are M.B. and B.S., which are classified Honours and Pass.

2. *The second degree is the Masters Degree.*

   The Masters Degree is awarded on the basis of examination by:

   (*a*) written papers; or

   (*b*) thesis or dissertation; or

   (*c*) written papers and thesis or dissertation.

   Sometimes an oral examination is required.

   A candidate for a Masters Degree must submit a thesis or dissertation if it is a part of the examination. The thesis or dissertation should be on work done in relation to the field of study; it must consist of the candidate's own account of his research.

3. *The third and final degree is the Doctorate of Philosophy, or Ph.D.*

   This is a research degree for which a thesis is required. Like the Masters, the thesis is submitted on completion of the study course and must be in written English. The Ph.D. thesis must form "a distinct contribution to the knowledge of the subject and afford evidence of originality shown either by the discovery of new facts or by the exercise of independent critical power. It must be satisfactory as regards literary presentation and must be suitable for publication".*

WHAT IS A THESIS?
A thesis is a written piece of work which is the result of research done in conjunction with a university course. It is completed in a specified time given by

---

* The University of the West Indies Calendar

the relevant faculty of the university. In the case of a Doctorate, the work must be literarily presentable and suitable for publication.

DIPLOMA

A diploma course is of at least one academic year in duration. On successful completion of the course a diploma is awarded. The minimum requirement for entrance to a diploma course is normally a general degree. All diploma examination papers are marked by external examiners.

CERTIFICATE

The status of graduate or the equivalent is not required for entry to a certificate course.

ACADEMIC ABBREVIATIONS

A.C.A.   Associate of the Institute of Chartered Accountants
A.C.I.I.   Associate of the Chartered Insurance Institute
A.C.I.S.   Associate of the Chartered Institute of Secretaries
A.I.B.   Associate of the Institute of Bankers
A.M.T.P.I.   Associate Member of the Town Planning Institute
A.R.A.M.   Associate of the Royal Academy of Music
A.R.C.A., A.R.C.M., A.R.C.O., A.R.C.S.   Associate of the Royal College of Arts, of Music, of Organists, of Science (respectively)
A.R.I.B.A.   Associate of the Royal Institute of British Architects
A.R.I.C.   Associate of the Royal Institute of Chemistry

B.A.   *(Baccalaureus Artium)* Bachelor of Arts
B.Agr.   Bachelor of Agriculture
B.A.Sc.   Bachelor of Applied Science
B.B.A.   Bachelor of Business Administration
B.Ch.   see Ch.B.
B.C.L.   Bachelor of Civil Law
B.Com.   Bachelor of Commerce
B.D.   Bachelor of Divinity
B.D.S.   Bachelor of Dental Surgery
B.Ed.   Bachelor of Education
B.Eng.   Bachelor of Engineering
B.F.A.   Bachelor of Fine Arts
B.L.   Bachelor of Law

B.Lit.   Bachelor of Literature
B.Litt.   Bachelor of Letters
B.M.   Bachelor of Medicine
B.Phil.   Bachelor of Philosophy
B.S.   Bachelor of Science (USA); Bachelor of Surgery (USA)
B.S.A.   Bachelor of Science Agriculture
B.Sc.   Bachelor of Science
B.Sc.D.   Bachelor of Science in Dentistry
B.S.C.E.   Bachelor of Science Civil Engineering
B.S.I.E.   Bachelor of Science Industrial Engineering
B.S.M.E.   Bachelor of Science Mechanical Engineering
B.Th.   Bachelor of Theology

C.A.   Chartered Accountant
C.D.A.   College Diploma in Agriculture
C.E.   Civil Engineer
Ch.B.   (*Chirurgiae Baccalaureus*) Bachelor of Surgery
Ch.M.   (*Chirurgiae Magister*) Master of Surgery
C.M.   Certified Master of Surgery
C.P.A.   Certified Public Accountant
C.P.H.   Certificate in Public Health

D.A.   Diploma in Anaesthesia
D.C.   Doctor of Chiropractics
D.C.H.   Diploma in Child Health
D.C.L.   Doctor of Civil Law
D.D.   Doctor of Divinity
D.D.S.   Doctor of Dental Surgery
D.I.C.T.A.   Diploma of the Imperial College of Tropical Agriculture
Dip.Arch.   Diploma in Architecture
Dip. Ed.   Diploma in Education
Dip.P.   Diploma in Planning
D.Lit.   Doctor of Literature
D.Litt.   Diploma in Letters
D.M.   Doctor of Medicine
D.Mus.   Doctor of Music
D.O.   Doctor of Opthalmology
D.P.A.   Diploma in Public Administration
D.P.H.   Diploma in Public Health
D.Phil.   Doctor of Philosophy
D.Sc.   Doctor of Science
D.Soc.   Doctor of Sociology

D.S.S.   Doctor of Sacred Scriptures
D.Th(eol).   Doctor of Theology
D.T.M.   Doctor of Tropical Medicine
D.T.M. & H.   Doctor of Tropical Medicine and Hygiene
E.D. Doctor of Engineering

F.A.A.P. Fellow of the American Association of Pediatrics
F.A.C.C.A Fellow of the Association of Certified and Corporate Accountants
F.A.C.Psych. Fellow of American College of Psychology
F.A.C.S. Fellow of American College of Surgeons
F.A.I. Fellow of the Chartered Auctioneer's Institute
F.A.I.A. Fellow of American Institute of Accountants
F.B.A. Fellow of the British Academy
F.B.O.A. Fellow of the British Optical Association
F.C.A. Fellow of the Institute of Chartered Accountants
F.C.W.A. Fellow of the Institute of Cost and Works Accountants
F.I.B. Fellow of the Institute of Bankers
F.I.E.R.E. Fellow of the Institute of Electrical and Radio Engineers
F.R.A.D., F.R.A.M. Fellow of the Royal Academy of Dancing, of Music
F.R.C.M., F.R.C.O., F.R.C.P. Fellow of the Royal College of Music,
    of Organists, of Physicians
F.R.C.O.G. Fellow of the Royal College of Obstetricians and Gynaecologists
F.R.C.S. Fellow of the Royal College of Surgeons
F.R.G.S. Fellow of the Royal Geographical Society
F.R.I.B.A. Fellow of the Royal Institute of British Architects
F.R.I.C. Fellow of the Royal Institute of Chemistry
F.R.I.P. Fellow of the Royal Institute of Pathology
F.R.S.M. Fellow of the Royal Society of Midwifery
F.R.S.S. Fellow of the Royal Statistical Society
F.R.S.T.M. Fellow of the Royal Society for Tropical Medicine

G.P. General Practitioner
Grad. I.C.E. Graduate of the Institute of Civil Engineers
Grad. I.E.E. Graduate of the Institute of Electrical Engineers
Grad. I.P. Graduate of the Institute of Physics

H.N.C. Higher National Certificate

J.C.D.   *(Juris Civilis Doctor)* Doctor of Civil Law
J.Dip.M.A.   Joint Diploma in Management Accounting
J.P.   Justice of the Peace

L.C.P. & S.   Licentiate of the College of Physicians and Surgeons
L.D.S.   Licentiate in Dental Surgery
Litt.D.   *(Litterarum Doctor)* Doctor of Letters
LL.B.   *(Legum Baccalaureus)* Bachelor of Laws
LL.D.   *(Legum Doctor)* Doctor of Laws
LL.M.   *(Legum Magister)* Master of Laws
L.R.C.P. & S.   Licentiate of the Royal College of Physicians and Surgeons
L.R.F.P. & S.   Licentiate of the Royal Faculty of Physicians and Surgeons
L.Th.   Licentiate in Theology

M.A.   Master of Arts
M.B.   *(Medicinae Baccalaureus)* Bachelor of Medicine
M.D.   *(Medicinae Doctor)* Doctor of Medicine
M.Ed.   Master of Education
M.I.E.J.   Member of the Institute of Engineers of Jamaica
M.O.M.   Medal of Merit (T'dad)
M.R.C.P.   Member of the Royal College of Physicians
M.R.C.S.   Member of the Royal College of Surgeons
M.S.   Master of Surgery
M.Sc.   Master of Science
M.Th.   Master of Theology

N.D.A. National Diploma in Agriculture

O.D. Doctor of Optometry

Ph.C. Pharmaceutical Chemistry
Ph.D. *(Philosophiae Doctor*) Doctor of Philosophy

Q.C. Queen's Counsel

S.C.M. State Certified Midwife
S.E.N. State Enrolled Nurse
S.R.N. State Registerd Nurse

T.D. Teacher's Diploma

V.S. Veterinary Surgeon

STARTING A CAREER

HINTS ON FINDING A JOB

Before you begin looking for a job, prepare a résumé of not more than one side of an A4 or foolscap paper. Divide it into four sections:

(*a*) Personal details (name, age, address and telephone number);
(*b*) Education;
(*c*) Experience;
(*d*) Skills.

Buy good quality stationery. Type all information except your signature. Do not use carbon copies of your résumé. Type each one or get it photocopied; keep a good supply of it.

Read the advertisements appearing in the daily papers or write to the company you are interested in working for. A covering letter must always accompany a résumé. When applying to a company which has not advertised, the letter should state the reasons for your interest in working for the company; ask if there is any vacancy or impending vacancy; and state the position you are most interested in but indicate your willingness to begin in another department if necessary. When replying to an advertisement, state the day, date and the publication in which it appeared. Unless a specific name is given, always address your application to the personnel manager.

Register with an employment agency but do not expect too much from it.

Never turn down an interview. Seek to change the date if it is excessively inconvenient, but not otherwise. Turn up at least five to ten minutes early.

When granted an interview, find out as much as possible about the company. Newspapers, the most recent annual report and the library are good sources.

Have two or three suitable questions to ask about the organization and how it is progressing (even if you know). For example: What is the most responsible position a woman can hold? What guidelines do you use in promoting employees and how many quick promotions have occurred recently?

Until you are short listed, do not discuss salary, fringe benefits, pension scheme, removal expenses and sports and social facilities.

On being given the job, make sure you are fully aware of your salary and salary reviews and all the benefits, if any. Do not rely on the advice of one man. Ask about the policy of staff assessment and how many people (apart from the directors) were given merit rises the year before.

HOW TO PREPARE YOURSELF FOR A JOB INTERVIEW

Before you get any job, you will be given an interview. That interview is probably the most important step in acquiring a job. So to help you along the way, here are some suggestions — ways in which you can prepare yourself beforehand for that decisive step into your future.

Know Yourself What are your interests and qualifications? Your prospective employer will want to know, so be prepared to talk about them briefly, intelligently and clearly during the interview.

Know Something About The Firm Before you go for the job interview, find out about the firm. The more you know about the firm the better you will be able to suggest ways you can be of service to your prospective employer when he interviews you.

Check Your Personal Appearance Before you leave for the interview, check your appearance. Be neat, clean, with hair combed, fingernails clean and shoes shined. Do not wear skin-tight jeans, slacks or a party dress; gaudy jewellery, heavy makeup and strong perfume.

Go To The Interview Alone The prospective employer is interested in you, in the way you present yourself. He does not want to hear what your relatives or friends think of you. He will judge for himself. So go to the interview alone.

Arrive Early Get to the interview a few minutes before time. Present yourself in a straightforward manner. Let the receptionist know who you are and whom you wish to see.

Be Alert During The Interview Sit up straight and look alert during the interview. Try to be at ease and to answer your prospective employer's questions in a business-like manner.

Think Before Answering Think before answering any question. Be polite, accurate, honest and frank. The employer is especially interested in the experience and training which you have had. So be prepared to answer questions such as these:

What work have you done?
How did you do it?
Did you use any special tools or equipment?
How much are you earning?
Have you done any volunteer work?
Do you have hobbies which might help you in a particular job?

Bring Your Résumé A fact sheet about your previous jobs — dates, salaries, kinds of work and reasons for leaving — is essential. You will be asked questions on these. So to save time, hand over your résumé.

Do Not Argue Be diplomatic, polite and tactful. Listen to everything the prospective employer has to say. Do not argue with him. Try to answer all his questions accurately and tactfully.

Leave Your Troubles At Home Do not tell the prospective employer your troubles. He is not interested in your personal or family problems. He is interested in you as a prospective employee.

Seek Advice As the interview ends, be cordial even though you feel you may not get the job. Seek the employer's advice on other jobs which may be available in the future. Make a good impression; he may call you back in the future.

WRITING YOUR RÉSUMÉ

Begin your résumé with the heading 'Personal'. Under it type your name, address, telephone number, age, marital status, height and weight. Include a head-and-shoulders photograph if you can, as recruiters find it helpful for identification purposes.

Under 'Education', name the schools you attended, your qualifications and the subject you specialize in. If you had any school honours, such as a scholarship, set them down.

Under 'Experience', describe your working experience in chronological order. List down the companies you have worked for, the dates of your employment and the positions held.

Mention any special skill you may have and a few of your hobbies or interests.

Do not try to be unique in your presentation. Keep your résumé business-like.

Check carefully for typographical errors or misspellings in your original résumé before making photostat copies.

Try to limit the length of your résumé to one page so that it does not necessitate extensive reading. Save further details for your personal interviews.

SAMPLE RÉSUMÉ

Carlton Rhoden

PERSONAL:

Address: *Mailing*
University of Technology
Hope Road,
Kingston 6
927-6154

Home
26 Duanvale Terrace,
Kingston
986-4948

Age: 20 years old Marital Status: Single

EDUCATION: Kingston College

GCE 'O' Level — English Language, Biology, Physics, Chemistry, Mathematics, Health Science (1972).

GCE 'A' Level — Physics, Chemistry, General Paper (1974).

Expecting a Diploma in Pharmacy at the end of present academic year.

EXPERIENCE: Summer Holiday Jobs.

1972 — Scientific Research Council, Research Assistant.

1973 — Bureau of Standards, Laboratory Assistant.

INTERESTS: Electronics, Football, Photography, Music.

REFERENCES: To be provided upon request.

SECTION EIGHT
DRUGS AND YOUR LIFE

DRUGS

A drug is a chemical which alters the way the mind or body works or which is used to treat an infection. Indeed, we all take drugs in one form or the other. The increasing availability and development of drugs have led to a situation which requires a new educational approach to the understanding of drug use. This is especially so as it is necessary to separate drug use into different categories.

Drug use invariably falls into three categories:
- Recreational
- Cultural
- Medicinal

Recreational use of drugs usually begins for the following reasons:
- It seems exciting
- Curiosity
- Peer pressure

Using drugs for recreation is common among the young as is manifested in the wide use of cocaine in the west. This contrasts with what takes place in the Caribbean and Latin America where marijuana and cocaine are often used for cultural purposes.

Drugs are most commonly used for medicinal purposes. Abuse in any of the drug-use categories above will almost certainly lead to addiction.

Addiction
Scientifically, it has been proven that the use of any drug for a period of 10 days exposes the body to some form of addiction (early tobacco advertisements successfully used this method [Camel Cigarettes and its 10 day tests]).

Not all drug users become addicts, but most do, even those who feel it cannot happen to them.

Addiction usually manifests itself in:
- Uncontrolled cravings
- Physical dependence
- Psychological dependence (needing drugs to engender a feeling of well being).

This can happen with tranquillizers, sleeping pills, alcohol and cigarette smoking, as well as cocaine and heroin.

Drug addiction also leads to:
- Behavioural changes
- Loss of appetite
- Wasted muscles
- Increased exposure to diseases such as hepatitis and AIDS.

MISUSED DRUGS AND THEIR EFFECTS

Amphetamines or speed: these stimulants make the user feel high and energetic, wide awake and lively; followed by a feeling of depression, irritability and the need for sleep.

Cannabis: comes from the plant *cannabis sativa* also called 'pot', 'hash', 'grass', 'weed', its most common effects are talkativeness, laughter, relaxation, and an awareness of brighter colours, and louder sounds. Regarded as a soft drug, there is little evidence of how harmful this drug is.

Cocaine: comes from the leaves of the Cocoa Shrub. Called 'snow' or 'white lady', it is a stimulant, giving energy, and confidence, followed by tiredness. 'Crack' is a derived form and is rapidly addictive.

LSD: Lysergic Acid Deethylamide — a powerful hallucinogen. When taken, it transports one to a different world where everything seems more intense. Light, sound, space and distance appear different. Use of this substance can increase the likelihood of accidents, and lead to mental illness.

Opiates: includes such drugs as opium, morphine, heroin, cocaine, methadone and pithidene; they are produced from the seeds of the opium poppy *'Paperver' Somniferum* but can be manufactured from chemically related substances. Their main effect is to reduce and relieve stress and discomfort. But they are considered hard drugs and very addictive.

Solvents: things such as lighter fuel, cleaning fuel and some glues produce a vapour which, when inhaled, depresses the activity of the nervous system, relieving anxiety. Solvents can damage the liver and the brain.

Effects on Sexual Life

Misuse of drugs can lead to sexual experimentation and promiscuity. Inevitably, this increases the chances of contracting sexually transmitted diseases. Drug abusers also tend to share needles, a practice which increases the spread of AIDS.

The dangers involved should be incentives to avoid abusing drugs. As one popular slogan goes, "Say No to Drugs".

www.ingramcontent.com/pod-product-compliance
Lightning Source LLC
Chambersburg PA
CBHW031512040426
42445CB00009B/192